Dreams Key to Our Soul

Rita Hawi

 www.trafford.com

North America & international
toll-free: 1 888 232 4444 (USA & Canada)
fax: 812 355 4082

First of all I want to wake up your interest for dreams by telling
my dream and realizing the deeper meaning that this dream my
unconscious wanted me to understand.
My dream is from 2001 and I remember that H.H Dalai Lama told
me to write it down.

I was driving in a wooden car over mountains up and down and I
enjoyed so much from fresh air and driving with a high speed.
Suddenly I came next to a torque colored sea and I saw my mother
sitting beside me.
I knew that I was next to Dead Sea and I continued to drive back
to the mountains and I saw a tunnel full of Roman Money. I saw
people coming and I took quickly some money with me and again
I found myself next to Dead Sea and my mother drove away with
her car to some other place and I stayed alone. I saw that the trail
where I have to drive will go under the water and I needed to check
everything very carefully that my car will not junk under the water
and I continued to drive again to the mountains. This time I found
a piece of Roman Glass and I was admired of the beautiful colors
and I just knew that the piece of Glass is much more valuable than
the money I found earlier and I hid it into my bag and I left the
mountains.

What happened to me in my waking life?

Less than 2 years later I and my family left Israel because of the
hard situation to abroad and 2 years later we came back and about
a year later I started to work in Qumran (next to the Dead Sea) and
my main work was to sell Roman Coins and Roman Glass. (Notice
that I have never seen in my life these items, I just knew the names
of these articles in my dreams). Once in the work I had little time
and I went to see the archeological area and I walked on the wooden
bridge and like a lightning I remembered my dream and I just knew
that there must be some reason that I am in this ancient place.
After one year I had to leave my work because of some problems
and a one year later I started to work there again and only for
the reason that I felt leaving there something valuable that I must
know.
Well, this time came a war and there was no work to anybody and I
was on my way to the mountains back to home.
This time it took only few days to realize the meaning of Roman
Glass and the beautiful colors.
The wooden car signifies my journey and really, at the first time
I got some money from sales of inheritance (Roman money
symbolizes euro) and my Mother passed away in this time (she left
me alone and drove to some other place), put the second time the
Ancient Roman Glass and the shiny colors symbolize my creation
and the result is this dream book.
Dreams are an ancient way to connect to our soul and the colors
symbolize my idea and finding my truth.

I want to add something very interesting!

In the beginning of August 2007 there has been a huge foundation
of Roman Coins and Roman Glass beside Qumran.
In the earlier years the Sea level was much higher, but because of
the global warming also Dead Sea becomes dry and somebody
walked beside the sea and found a Roman Coin and they started to
look more of these items.
(I saw a trial where I have to drive will go under the water . . .) In
2001 the foundation was still under the water!

This picture is from Dead Sea from Qumran

We all sleep about 1/3 of our life; put do we really know what is going on with us during our sweet dreams?

To see dreams is the most natural way to connect to our soul and dreams can tell us much more than we can imagine. Sometimes we only dream of symbols and sometimes we get clear messages. It is a very individual and secret world and we only have to learn how to analyze them.

First of all it is necessary for our brainwork, because during dreams we allow for our brains to keep some kind of balance between body and mind. Even blind people can feel during their dreams smells and emotions like most people do. I have read that people who don't remember dreams will be nervous and neurotic.

3

Also it is very healthy to see dreams, except our muscles will rest and protein and building hormones will renew (our brains get order to create these hormones when we are sleeping).

We all remember Josef from the Old Testament, I thing he was the first famous person who knew to understand and explain dreams from symbols which appear in dreams. The symbols have been changed by the years according to our education and surroundings, but most of the ancient symbols have still the same meaning, they have not changed. Only our understanding, sometimes very wrong (like the Swastika) has been changed.

Much later there was a man called Sigmund Freud and he gave us new psychoanalytical ideas; relationships between the past and the day we live. Dreams can be from everyday life and sometimes we can even solve problems that are worrying us in our waking life. Here you have a nice sample that I solved to one woman.

I was with my boyfriend and I steeled from my fathers desk 8 batteries, because I needed them so badly and later on I felt bad because of I took this batteries without asking permission from him and now I want to know what this kind of dream can tell to me?

My answer:

Why did you take energy so much from your father and of cause you felt bad, because you didn't want even to ask permission from him and the 8 symbolizes something that you took from him.

Her answer:

I feel so confused; I took 8000 Euro from him, because I am unemployed and didn't want advices from him. (Batteries signify to energy and steel symbolizes in this case not to ask permission and advices).

I don't agree with C. G. Jung that we can't dream of our future. I have collected dreams from many people from different parts of the world; even with different languages that person does not understand in waking life. The most famous dream was from Abraham Lincoln that he saw his murderer in his dream from future. I have good sample from my daughter, she was only 6 years old, and this time she spoke only Hebrew and few words in English. She dreamed of my brother from abroad, he told to her in her dream; good bye Helen, I am now in the heaven.

In the morning she told me this dream and asked me what means heaven. Same day I got a phone call from abroad that my brother has passed away. I agree with astrology that planets have a strong influence to our dreams. I saw my life dream when Mercury trine natal Uranus was transiting according my birth map. One night before a well known astrology send me this e-mail:

Einstein had a lot of days like this. The metaphorical light bulb pops on your head-so what if it 3 o'clock in the night, get up and write it down. Important stuff infiltrates your grey matter-seeking black and white definition, comply the gifts of brilliance that universe offers you. You get answers with flash of intuition.

About 3.20 am I woke up and wrote my dream down. It was an incredible experience.

Also except moon, planets like Uranus, Neptune and Pluto are connected to intuitive dreams.

We can see also dreams from our past life and usually there is a reason. These kinds of dreams can continue several times. I have got a nice sample from Europe.

One woman dreamt few times that she is falling down from a mountain and she was very afraid from high places in her waking life and how she dreamt of one of her soul circulation:

She was a small child and she was climbing with her mother on the mountains. She remembered that they had long dresses and they were looking after food. Beside her was a deep valley and she stepped on a small stone, lost her balance and felt down to the valley. Next morning everything was clear to her and she realized her fears to high places.

Sometimes we dream of death and then it really happens. I believe that these kinds of dreams are forewarning us, put same time the dream can prepare us to survive from the shock.

But sometimes these kind of dreams only indicates long life to the person we dreamt about. I have other kind of message somebody gave me from internet:

She was a young student in Paris far away from her parents who were living in Finland.

She didn't have contact with them for a long time and one night she dreamt about the end of the world and everything was ruined around her.

In the morning she decided to phone her parents and she got the very hard message that her father has died suddenly in the same night.

The messages can be also from unconscious and I have a very good example from Europe:

Her dream about birds:

I saw a dream that somebody threw arrows, put the arrows were like white birds and I knew that they wanted to give me a message, put I couldn't understand it. After those two little birds attacked my throat, I only remember that the birds were green and I felt choked and tried to chase the birds away.

Later I dreamed of a bear and the bear was sleeping beside a lake and some waves wet the bear.

My analyzing to her dream:

Birds really bring messages, like the white birds in your dream put you couldn't understand what they wanted from you. The birds wanted to make the message clearer and they attacked your throat; the green bird symbolizes your throat, communications—the green charka is connected to communications. What is not working with your communication? I think the bear makes your dream clearer, bear symbolizes your famine aspect and the water signifies emotions. If I understood your dream; the birds really brought a message—you should learn to show more your emotions.

She just answered me." You are absolutely right and I have really a problem to show my emotions and it caused by my childhood days".

Nowadays the most typical dreams are:

Running away (afraid of something)

To be naked in a public place (secret from the private life that you don't want others to know).

Flying (signifies the feeling of freedom).

Nightmares (indicates chaos in your waking life).

Numbers of these dreams are clear to us, for example why we are afraid, what kind of problem is worrying you in your waking life: work loss, lack of money, and love.

Secrets from private life, of course we try to hide them from surroundings, put our unconscious symbolizes these fears as-to be naked.

During our dreams unconscious is releasing emotions and same time collecting new energy and here you can read how you can release emotions;

"I had a difficult operation about 2 years ago and since then I have been only at home. Me and my family have had a hard times during my operation.

Last night I again dreamt a real nightmare; I dreamt that my legs were transparent, without any muscles, I only saw the bones and veins and my knee was crushed.

Later on in the same night my dream continued. I was so afraid of my daughter and she was jumping and raging and finally she fell down. I called to her, put she didn't want to listen and she run away.

Few weeks earlier I dreamt that my hands were transparent and I was so afraid.

My answer to her:

Your situation must be confusing; the question is if you want to change your life. Try
to create muscles to your legs and hands, at least it will help to heal
your soul, just try to concentrate hard and have patient and try to
do these exercise just before you go to
Sleep.

Your daughter is young and healthy and has full of vitality-that is why she didn't want to listen to you. You have to wipe your fears away, because your fears are also disturbing your healing process. Your dream was clear forewarning from your unconsciousness to be aware of your healthy.

All our history has stories from people and their dreams; bible I believe is one of the most famous books that have so many good samples.

Personally I like Augustinian and his vision that dreams are connection between us, angels and God (body, mind and spirit)

I also believe to Freud's claim that our secret desires comes true at least in our dreams. Jung continued Freud's claim and found out that secret desires can come true at least in our dreams (lacks in reality).

You can have also other kind of dreams, feeling or need for something, feeling of hunger or you want to eat something and you are not able to get it. This kind of dream happened to my friend when she was abroad and pregnant. She wanted to eat something special from Armenia and she couldn't get this food. In the night she just dreamt of that food and she ate and ate . . . After she waked up in the morning she didn't want to eat this food anymore Artist can dream of paintings. Surrealistic Bosch and Goya are maybe the most famous artist Here you can see my surrealistic painting and this picture is from my dreams.

A rising moon

During our sleep we have 5 about 30 minutes long light REM (rapid eye movement) and in REM dreams it is very easy to remember the dreams. They are usually connected to emotions and REM dreams are like large memory card of computer (even from the earlier soul circulations) that gives us reactions to our dreams (reactions you can understand like learnt lessons).

Time when it is NREM (non rapid eye movement) we are in deep sleep. I can say that if we couldn't the solve problem in REM-level, we can continue to solve it in NREM-level, because after this kind of dream we automatically will ask solution for a problem from our mind.

Why we dream night mares? S, Freud claims that they are unfilled desires. I personally believe that there is a problem if this kind of dreams continue, and advice to go to professional help, it is a chaos situation.

Telepathy is also connected to dreams and here you have a nice sample: One girl got a nice jewelry box from her father as a present from abroad. Day after the girlfriend of this jewelry box owner came to visit her and show the present that her girlfriend's father gave her. Her friend came pale and she told to her that last night she dreamt of same jewelry box as she got a present Jung claims also that sometimes our conscious mind is not aware from unconscious, some aspects of yourself and here you can read a very nice sample from a woman from Scandinavia. She is a bi-sexual put she has hidden this aspect of herself during all her life and nowadays she is a very famous artist.

Her dream:
I saw a dream of a wizard that I so loved and anyhow the wizard judged me because I am a bi-sexual put without him I couldn't realize my reality and illusion.
For me the wizard was like a guardian angel. So, he was in my dream and he came to visit me with his daughter, put his daughter wanted to go to the city and after all he let her go.
All the time he was worried of her and I suggest him to go for an evening walk and in the same way we can find his daughter.
The wizard used to be a very shy person and I was very surprised that he started to knock doors of strangers and anyhow I followed him to the house.
First of all we went to a hall and then to the bedroom and I saw a very small bed and I asked him how he has place to sleep in so small bed?
He answered to me, quite comfortable, put only for sleeping.
Somebody brought us a glass of red juice and we thank the lady and we continued to walk to the living room.
I saw big windows covered with lace curtains and lot of palm trees.
I noticed a sofa
And the wizard was sitting with his daughter on the sofa. She was sitting on his knees and laughing all the time and she was so happy when the wizard told her that she is his small beauty.
We all continued our journey to a new house and there was only one room. The walls were from gold and I noticed o'clock, it was sight to number 2, I realized that there must a meaning for

the number, put I couldn't understand it. We left the house and I saw my teacher friend and she was a pit down and told me from her boarding life. I wanted to ask her to come with us, put after all I didn't because I knew that she didn't want to knock doors of strangers and we left her alone.

We started to walk away from the city and suddenly came a motorcycle with very high speed and almost killed us put we succeeded to jump to the side of the road.

I asked the wizard where we are going now.

He told me with a very peaceful voice that he knew a short way to home.

We went to a tunnel and I found myself at home.

This is her answer to her dream:

I understood that the wizard is one aspect of me (masculine). Even the wizard was a very shy person put his soul was not at all. I never could go and knock doors of unknown people.

On the other hand I understood that the small bed symbolized my need to have a famine partner-put I never allowed it to myself. In the small bed was place enough for my soul to rest.

Red juice indicates my accepting from the environment and the golden wall signifies higher understanding and the clock took a long time to me until I understood it.

Number 2 symbolizes a bi-sexual and that I need to find balance as soon as possible.

Motorcycle represents my need to decide alone of my life or otherwise others will drive on me. Short way symbolizes the spiritual home and where I can find balance.

I must say that this lovely lady understands herself perfectly. (That is why she is an artist).

As I told you earlier that you can solve problems in your dream, only you need to ask the solution from yourself before sleeping.

The people who study Kabala for years, also they, like we all have the everyday problems that are worrying them and they have very special way to solve their worries.

Before they go to sleep they ask from themselves that they can find an answer to a problem that is worrying them. They know to power of unconscious and usually they get statements from kabala and this is an other way to understand your dreams.

Also ESP, extra sensory perception, it is a situation that dreams will happen later on,

Of course with the language of symbols, depending of culture and mostly how well the person knows himself.

ASC, catered stages of consciousness, is a situation that you are in deep meditation.

You can have even mysterious experience.

Many people keep a notebook of their dreams and many of dreamers have noticed

Later on how correct their dreams have been

Last thing is the Deja Vu—feeling that you have been in same situation. The dream bobs out later on, almost everybody has been in this kind of situation. Earlier Deja Vu and epilepsy was connected together because many patients of epilepsy have more Deja Vu phenomenon.

There are no limits how do you dream and we, our self are the best under standers and we only have to learn how to analyze the symbols.

Remember to pay attention to the emotions and try to find out the hidden message from your dreams.

You are the only one who knows your past; it is your memory card. This is the real co operation with your soul and you can understand your needs and your personal life much better and as I told to you, even to solve problems. I can give you only one advice before you go to sleep—Try to thing positive matters; it helps to change our life better!

I have collected for years the most typical symbols and the symbols are up date to modern life from very different parts of the world and religions. Because we all understand that in North America and from Africa the same symbols are not simply working, because of the different culture and the very different life style.

So, let's start to build the puzzle.

A

Abandonment symbolizes choked emotions.

Abduction—you are waiting for unexpected news.

Abject signifies financial change.

Above signifies your lack of faith.

Abscond—are you ashamed of morally reasons?

Abduct-are you lending ideas of somebody else?

Abroad signifies unbalance to your current situation.

Abscess signifies your need to express feelings.

Absorb indicates ability to integrate different situations.

Abuse signifies false friends.

Abyss—try to control your hidden fears.

Academy symbolizes new opportunities.

Accelerator signifies loss of control.

Acceptance—you are waiting acceptance to your decision.

Accident signifies hard life style.

Account—your energy is about the same with your bank account.

Accumulate-It depends if the accumulate is empty or full. Full accumulate signifies good luck.

Act signifies that you have an ability to see your life with the eyes of others.

Accuse signifies your guilty feelings.

Adder snakes symbolizes health, wisdom and sex (Christians believe that the snake symbolizes the sin of Adam and Eva).

Address-try to remember what has happen in the address you dreamt?

Adoption-your wishes will come true with a help of others.

Adulterate signifies the money problems that you try to solve (not always in the honest way)

Aircraft signifies too much high targets; flying in a airplane signifies your success to reach the goals.

Flying in common signifies to renew your energies and to relax.

Altar symbolizes responsibility. I f you are standing before an altar, maybe you are planning to marry?

Ambulance—if you see an ambulance full of wounded people signifies death and violent.

Gypsies believe if you see an ambulance signifies fulfillment of your desires.

Amok run—maybe you are realizing your hard emotions in your dream.

Ancestor signifies journey to the past.

Angel is a good sign-symbolizes luck in love, good friendship and new business opportunities.

In Christianity an angel symbolizes innocent and purity. An angel can also be a guardian angel during your life.

Anchor signifies strong connection to some person, if the rope is cut signifies lost of friendship. If the anchor is under water signifies disappointments.

Gypsies claim that if you see an anchor-your business will run better and if you lift the anchor signifies good profit.

Animals—many people dream of animals.

Usually if you run away from wild animals signifies worries in your waking life.

If you are afraid of animals signifies worries in your waking life. If you eat meat of animals signifies that your vitality will grow. Pets usually symbolize need of tender.

Annihilate signifies a loss or end of everything.

Ant is a symbol of order and diligent. Promote the important work.

Antics indicate need to prove yourself, you don't trust your talents.

Antique signifies good decision in earlier times. Some desires from past can appear to your head.

Antler is connected to sexuality and masculine power.

Apartment is a picture of your personality.

Bedroom signifies your intimae life

Kitchen signifies your avenges and warmness.

Sitting room is the Centrum of society.

Cellar is connected to unconsciousness

Garret is a symbolic of your soul.

Apple is usually connected to sexuality-like to taste something forbidden. In Christianity signifies the sin of Adam and Eva. Apple is also connected to temptation.

Application signifies changes. If your partner is filling an application signifies difficulties.

Apricot signifies good health.

Arbor—green leaves symbolizes creation, luck, success and vitality.

Archbishop signifies promotion from a person that is in a higher position than you are.

I f you see him in black clothes signifies danger in the night.

Archipelago foretells that two hermit souls can find each others.

Aroma—from the smell of aroma you can find out your feelings.

Army—if you are in the army signifies straight order personality.

Army usually signifies or danger or security.

Ash signifies loss and unlucky.

Ashamed—you are feeling sorry of something you have done.

Assemblage signifies balance between your soul and surroundings

Assistant—you don't like changes in your life, if someone else is your assistant signifies promotion in your work.

Atom bomb signifies chaos in your personal situation.

Attack—Do you want to defend yourself or has somebody violated you?

Auction I f you have organized on auction, you have hand over your property, if you are purchasing a property—you have to build your future again

Audience signifies need for attention.

Augur foretells an important message, especially if you have numbers or animals as a symbolic. Aurora signifies an inspiration.

Auto signifies yourself, how do you drive and where do you drive. Gypsies believe

That driving with a car signifies financial improvement and if you overtake other cars

Signifies a good business opportunities.

If you are buying a new car signifies good offer for a new work.

Avarice—do you want too much from the other people? It is a strongly negative symbol.

Avenue signifies your need to re-fresh yourself.

B

Baboon you are expressing yourself in unusual matter.
Baby signifies a new life or a new idea.
Baby carriage signifies surprise from a good friend.
Baby clothes—are you expressing yourself in subtle way?
Baby sitter signifies your need to take care of child within yourself.
Back-Biting signifies family problems.
Back Gammon Unwelcome quest is coming soon.
Back packing signifies survival skills.
Backward what ever you are seeking in life appears to be moving away from you
Back yard signifies childhood memories.
Bacon is a symbolic of life's supply.
Bad signifies balance-off, worthless emotions.
Bachelor-Be careful with your love affairs.
Back signifies uncontrolled situation, somebody is putting stress on you. Badger signifies sorrow.
Bag is connected to sexuality. In your handbag you can keep all your secrets.
Badminton you need to decide for some opportunities.
Baggage are usually heavy, put what to do, life is not always easy.
Bake is always a good sing. From food you get the vitality for the life.
Bake house signifies danger and pitfalls.
Bagel the key element is missing in your life.
Bagpipe signifies good luck.
Bail symbolizes that you need help with your business dealings.
Bar mitzvah signifies sense of morality.
Barbarian is an instinctual aspect of your character.
Barbie doll signifies your desire to leave your responsibilities to others.
Barefoot signifies carefree attitude and good understanding.
Bargain indicates that you are being under valued.
Bark maybe you are barking others instead of talking friendlier.

Bar if you are drinking beside a bar desk signifies new plans. Gypsies forewarn that to drink alcohol in a bar signifies false friends. If you are drinking together with a friend signifies to control your passion.

Barley signifies good health and wealth.

Barn it depends what kind of condition is the barn; good condition signifies your knowledge to control emotions and bad condition signifies that you don't know how to control your feelings.

Barrel you can feel save in a barrel if you feel some danger.

Basement is a symbolic of your unconscious, there you can keep memories, and afterwards you can remember them and accept yourself in a new way.

Basin symbolizes female love.

Baseball if you are playing baseball represents peace of mind.

Basil to smell or taste basil refers deep love.

Basketball signifies need for co-operation and assistance of others.

Bath indicates ridding yourself from old ideas. If you are bathing with someone you are seeking for a closer connection with that person.

Bathrobe is a symbol of purification.

Basket if the basket is broken symbolizes difficulties and if you see many baskets your targets are blessed.

Bat signifies problems with deceitful person.

Bat ion symbolizes male sexuality or power.

Battle if you are attractive you trust your spiritual power.

Bauble symbolizes need to get attention.

Bawl if you are bawling you need to ask help from others to your trouble put if you are bawling from happiness signifies good luck.

Bayonet somebody wants to hurt you with harmful words

Beach signifies changes in your life, sea usually signifies deep emotions, power that you have inside put in beach you find balance between earth and water.

Beans signify your roots and humanity.

Bear is usually a symbolic of maternal love put signifies also to masculine power.

Bead symbolizes unpleasant life.

Beam sometimes is troubling to your mind—on the other hand it is an optimistic symbol because you are leaving your past and new things are waiting for you.

Beard long beard symbolizes luck and power. If you wash your beard signifies sorrow.

If a woman gets a beard, her secret desire will come true.

Bearing signifies need to self emphasize.

Beat signifies ignorance.

Beaver symbolizes ambition.

Bed symbolizes to make love or maybe it is comfortable to run away under the blanket from worries that you don't know how to solve.

Bed wetting signifies lack of control in your life.

Bedspread signifies your open sexuality.

Bedroom is a symbolic of your intimae life.

Beehive you have many opportunities just beside you and also symbolize teamwork.

Bee is a symbolic of systematic and a hard working person-is it true?

Beer signifies vitality and self-indolence.

Beg usually the beiger is the dreamer. It signifies unhappiness in your life and need to be alone.

Behead you are punishing too much yourself—put anyhow signifies new life.

Bell when the bells are ringing in your dream signifies need to prove yourself something "attention everybody". Gypsies believe that if you hear the bells of a church resound foretells of enemies and to hear bells foretells bad news.

Benzene gypsies believe that benzene signifies gossip and false friends.

Besom signifies that you try to hide your past.

Betoken there is always way to solve problems, what did you dream, animals, numbers or maybe the real true?

Belt signifies issues of morality.

Bench suggest that you should take more innovative role in your life

Bending signifies your ability to adapt yourself to new situations.

Beryl symbolizes hope and happiness.

Betrayal represents your suspicion about particular person or a situation

Bewilderment-are you stuck between two opposing views?

Bible symbolizes the truth, belief, inspiration and knowledge.

Bicycle-you need more balance between work and pleasure in order to have success.

Big-to see big figure in your dream represents authority and power.

Bigamy-it is difficult in weighting your opinions and make decision between them.

Billboard symbolizes a sign or a message that you need to notice in your bath in order to get your targets.

Billiards represents your compete nature.

Bikini maybe you feel unprotected emotionally.

Binoculars-you need to weight some situation again before you make a decision.

Bird chiding or flying birds symbolizes joy and happiness. To dream of dead bird foretells sorrow and disappointments.

Bird eggs symbolize money.

Birdhouse you should give more attention to your spiritual life.

Birdhouse is a symbol of spring

Birth represents start of new life. If a woman dreams of a birth signifies success.

Bite is usually connected to sexuality.

Black-do you feel your life a bit useless?

Blackhead signifies need for a change.

Black Marketer—do you try to hide something?

Blackout-what is wrong with you, do you feel danger or feeling useless?

Try to find light to your life.

Blade—it is a good sign, green blade symbolizes vitality, good. Luck and it is time to create. If the blade is falling down signifies that you are sorry for something.

Blanket symbolizes comfort; it is easy to run away under the blanket from all the world.

Blare do others really pay any attention even you are blaring.

Blaspheme-maybe you are blaspheming some aspect of yourself what you don't like so much.

Blazer is a social symbol.

Blazon-do you really need attention?

Bleed signifies temporally illness.

Bless—maybe you are blessing a new idea.

Blind-you can't find the right way this moment or you are not sure of your future, there is a concrete problem.

Blizzard signifies new power to create something.

Block-you should find a way out from the block, because some situation needs to be changed, if you manage to find a way your problems will disappear.

Blood is a symbolic of Christianity, balance between the body and the soul.

Blossom symbolizes vitality and happiness. To pick up a flower signifies that your desire will fulfill. If you smell a flower you will find a new love. Broken flower forewarns of sorrow. If you plant flowers foretells that you are doing great work.

Blouse signifies your personality. What are the colors and quality of your blouse?

Blow out—there will be any support to your new idea.

Blue Jacket signifies new fresh emotions.

Blue is a strong spiritual color.

Blunder forewarns not to make the same mistake again.

Blush signifies a strong active passion.

Boarding House signifies need for a rest.

Boat Rile-you are blowing with strong energies and are active to reach your goals.

Bomb is forewarning you to take care of your health.

Bound somebody is disturbing you to go forward, or maybe it is your work. Open the bound you will have a great future.

Bone you don't enjoy of your partner "only the bones are left".

Book—Try to notice the name and the message of the book you dreamt. If you dreamt of many books signifies rich spiritual life. If you have many picture in the book signifies your trust to hard work.

Boot—there is a limit between your movements and rights.

Bought symbolizes your roots, what more bought you have that better will be the tree.

It signifies your warm relationship with your family.

Bounty symbolizes need to be accepted.

Broadest-your desire will be fulfilled.

Box-you dreamt about a kit that is inside you.

Bracelet usually jewelry symbolizes good, pay attention if you have any stones in your bracelet or if it is from gold or silver.

Brains signify your ability to solve problems. Do you feel that you can do everything

Or are your brains useless?

Branch is usually connected to family tree and how warm are the relationship. If the branch has broken it is not a good sing.

Brave-if you are brave in your dream (as well others) symbolizes a strong character.

Break symbolizes difficulties. Gypsies believe if you have broken furniture or dishes at home symbolize hard times in business. A broken bottle signifies illness.

Breathe when you notice that you are breathing in your dream signifies strong healthy energies around you.

Brisk if you are a brisk in your dream signifies your life vitality

Brittle symbolizes loosing vitality.

Brook signifies happiness

Broom signifies that you are "cleaning your life".

Brother-maybe you have a competition with your brother. If the brother is older than you are signifies that an older person is against you or your views. Alternatively signifies disharmony between two aspects, the good and the bad.

Bruise indicates change of personality.

Brutal is also a symbolic of personality.

Bulb signifies a fruitful plan and it is also a symbolic of hard work, put then you also have results of your work.

Bullet if a bullet passes you symbolizes success.

Bumper it is also a good sing, your targets are successful.

Bunch your secret desire will be fulfilled.

Bungalow maybe you need a holiday and your soul needs to rest.

Burden symbolizes the experience of the life. Maybe the burden is too heavy and you need someone to carry it with you.

Bureau symbolizes memories and everyday routines.

Burial Gypsies believe that if you dream of burial signifies that you will see an old friend and if you are in the burial signifies a loss of good friend.

If you will be buried signifies long life.

Business signifies to satisfy the basic needs and to do the business correct.

Bust is a symbolic of mother and sex.

Butcher is a religious symbolic, signifies need to grow up, on the other hand maybe you feel quilt for a mistake and that is why you are on "the hands of butcher.

Butterfly symbolizes the soul. Do you want somebody catch your soul?

Bottom symbolizes false. If the bottoms are open signifies that you are afraid of something.

Buy if you pleased with your shopping signifies that you are happy with the decision you have made and if not signifies your undertaking.

C

Cap maybe you need to ask some advice from other person before moving forward.

Cabbage suggest not to waste time for nothing.

Cabin success comes only from your own contribution.

Cable represents durability.

Cackle symbolizes illness and loss.

Cactus symbolizes need to defend yourself in some way.

Caduceus suggests taking care of your health.

Café Tina denotes that lot of worries are eating you up inside.

Cage symbolizes being able to overcame your fears.

Cake symbolizes happiness, joy of family and friends. If you are baking a cake signifies your ability to solve problems. If the cake is decorated and has candles denotes success in your work.

Calamitous signifies you try to avenge yourself from some kind of fail.

Calculate signifies that you are not sure of your future.

Calf symbolizes inexperience.

Calomel signifies manipulation used by your lover.

Calves signify that you will enter soon to love relationship that may be depending on you.

Calendar signifies memories from the past or maybe you have to notice some important dates.

Calf symbolizes personality of youngster.

Call you need help from other person to solve your troubles.

Calm small problems can't unshake you.

Camel signifies problems that you are caring on your shoulders.

Camera—do you need to take a picture from yourself? Signifies need to check your own personality; sometimes it is good to do it, because you can see yourself in a objective way.

Camp-signifies needs to be alone or need to have change.

Candidacy signifies new possibilities.

Campfire signifies sharing and your need for companionship.

Camping signifies your need for more touch with nature.

Campus—need to challenge yourself mentally.

Can—Are you hiding something from your past that you need to hold on and pestle?

Can Opener signify your willingness to accept new ideas?

Canal—you are holding too much resistance from other people.

Canary signifies harmony and happiness.

Candle symbolizes vitality and romance. If the candle light are off signifies disappointments.

If a woman dreams a candle to light on signifies propose a marriage.

If a man dreams a candle to light on signifies money.

Many candle lights symbolize celebration.

Cannibal signifies self ruining power.

Capital symbolizes the world around you. If you are in a new city signifies changes for your daily life. If you don't know the places signifies that you don't like changes.

Captain-You will get better work or promotion.

Candy symbolizes joy, sensuality and pleasure.

Canyon symbolizes your unconscious and hidden messages.

Captive signifies celebration for some reason.

Capture gives vitality for the soul.

Car symbolizes our personality, how you control the driving, feelings when you drive, if there are brooks on your way indicates problems with your health, if someone drives on you signifies you to be careful of that person has caused the accident. Gypsies believe when you drive a car foretells you coming rich and if cars are passing you on the road your business will grow up. If you are buying a new car forewarns of loosing something valuable and if you are selling a car foretells getting a good work offer.

Carbon symbolizes lot of power and burning carbon symbolizes love and to shovel carbons symbolizes money.

Cards-playing cards: red cards symbolize love and happiness and black cards symbolize sorrow and illness. Red clubs signifies happiness and be beloved and black heart forewarns of unhappy marriage. Spade signifies troubling times ahead.

Carnival represents falsehoods; you need harmony in your life.

Carpenter indicates your overcoming obstacles. Carpet represents your way to protect yourself and your realities, also a symbolic of richness.

Carriage signifies your way of thinking is out of order.

Carrot symbolizes abundance.

Carry-Maybe you feel a burden to somebody?

Cartoon-It is good to know to laugh at yourself.

Casa Register symbolizes financial worries.

Casino signifies a risk taker within you.

Castle signifies reward, honor and need for protection.

Castration signifies overwhelming fears that you have lost feeling of sexual pleasure, also signifies lack of creativity.

Cat signifies misfortune, put for cat lover signifies feminine sexuality.

Caterpillar symbolizes your personal growth.

Cattle signify need for joy.

Cauldron signifies transformation.

Cave symbolizes unconscious. Gypsies believe if you stand beside a cave, a good friend deceives you.

CD symbolizes need for joy.

CD player symbolizes inspiration and signifies pleasure of listening music.

Ceiling represents mental perspective.

Celebration represents higher lever of growth. It is also a symbolic of freedom and emotional release.

Celery signifies need to be cleaned physically and emotionally.

Ceil Phone represents your mobility.

Cellar represents your subconscious mind-where the fears and problems are hidden.

It is our memory card.

Cello signifies creative achievements.

Cemetery signifies rebirth and sadness. Gypsies believe that cemetery signifies happy family ceremonies.

Centipedes-You need to stop thinking negatively.

Cereal signifies starting of new project.

Ceremony signifies sacrifice.

Certificate indicates to seek validity and truth to some situation.

Chains symbolizes need to brake free from routine. Gypsies believe than a chain foretells good news in the near future.

Chainsaw signifies that something drastic is about to happen.

Chair-First of all sit and thing, and then it is a time for proceeding.

Chalice signifies for spiritual nourishment.

Chalkboard-Do you have difficult times in the school, signifies your depth.

Chameleon signifies your ability to adapt new situations.

Champagne is a symbolic of sexuality.

Chanting symbolizes elevated sense of spiritually.

Charcoal signifies burning passion.

Char bracelet is a symbolic of protection of any harm.

Cheap represents your own feelings of inadequacy.

Cheating-To dream that you are cheating at the game signifies that you are not honest with yourself.

Check-Maybe you feel indebted to others. It is also a symbolic of unusual potential.

Checkerboard symbolizes facets of your own personality.

Checks symbolize commitment and closeness and your strength of character.

Cheerleader symbolizes competition.

Cheese symbolizes profits.

Chemicals signify transformation and individual process.

Cherry is a symbolic of honest and signifies good luck.

Cherub signifies innocent and need to take life more easily.

Chess signifies your character and your need to thing carefully before making any movement.

Chest signifies vitality.

Chickens symbolize cowardliness. Gypsies believe that chickens are a symbolic of False.

Chihuahua represents someone around who is unexpectedly vocal.

Childhood indicates your wish to return to the life without any responsibilities and worries.

Children signify your need to feel needed.

Chili signifies raw emotions. If you are wandering in a chili field signifies your emotions that you should be worried; unwanted sex or a life situation that needs urgent change.

Chimera signifies feeling of confusion

Chimney symbolizes tradition and family values.

Chocolate signifies self reward.

Choir signifies spiritual harmony.

Choking—If you are choking in your dream on an object that you will find hard to swallow or difficult to accept.

Christ represents perfection of self and spiritual truth.

Christmas symbolizes family unit and traditions.

Christmas tree symbolizes gathering and familiar relationship, also self development.

Chrome signifies growing vitality.

Chrysanthemums represent abundance and humanity.

Church signifies nourishment and, maybe you are looking for some spiritual guidance.

Churning symbolizes chaos and disorder.

Cigar represents luxury and relaxed stage of mind.

Cigarette-If you are smoking a cigarette in your dream signifies need for a break.

Circle symbolizes wholeness, alternatively signifies that you are protected.

Circus symbolizes your contentment with your surroundings.

Citrine is a gemstone that symbolizes good luck in business and your personal power.

City signifies sense of community and social environment.

Clam-You need to show more your feelings.

Class signifies stress with your studies. Also signifies the past lesson that you have learned.

Classroom is a symbolic of a life.

Claws signifies to be careful with your words and action

Clay is a symbolic of healing.

Cleaners signify you to clean up your emotional out burns.

Cleaning symbolizes that you are cleaning the negative energies out from your life.

Cliff indicates increased level of understanding.

Climb Ladder symbolizes to overcame a struggle. If you are climbing down signifies need to notice of your unconscious. To walk under a ladder signifies bad luck.

Clock signifies need for security. What you have done and what you didn't have time enough, if it is time to speed your actions. A clock symbolizes ticking of human heart.

Closed signifies an opportunity that is closed off to you.

Closet symbolizes an unveiling of hidden aspects of you.

Cloth represents pieces that compose your life.

Clothing symbolizes how people see you in public, your character and your way of thinking. What colors you are matching together and what is quality of your clothes.

If the clothes are new signifies new attitude and if the clothes are torn or ripped denotes some flaws in your thinking. To buy new clothes signifies need to be well-suited to your role.

Clouds signify inner peace. To dream of gloomy clouds signifies depression and anger.

Clover-To see a hand clover foretells good luck.

Clown symbolizes the child inside you.

Club symbolizes combativeness

Clubbing represents sense of belonging.

Clumsy-Don't make the things hard for yourself.

Coal represents wealth and prospers.

Coast symbolizes a metaphor for how to coast through the life.

Coat symbolizes your protectiveness and a fur coat symbolizes luxury. If you are wearing a fur coat signifies that you feel down yourself.

Cobra signifies creative energies.

Cobwebs-You are not utilizing your talents and potential.

Colane-Are you feeling empty and devoid of emotions.

Coconuts signify unexpected gift or money.

Cocoon represents healing or transformation.

Coffee-If you are drinking a coffee in your dream signifies need to slow down or maybe you are acting too hasty. Coffee signifies also hospitality and sharing of knowledge.

Coins symbolizes missed opportunity that came your way, if you are flipping a coin signifies that you are not taking a responsibility for your decisions.

Cold signifies being isolated. On the other hand the dream may occur as a result of your immediate environment in which you really are feeling cold.

Collapse-Don't push yourself too hard.

Collar symbolizes frustrating work or relationship.

Collage-Are you going through some social or cultural changes?

Colorless signifies feeling of sorrow.

Colors signify vitality and emotions.

Colt signifies feeling of insecure.

Column symbolizes hard work.

Coma-You feel helpless in some given situation.

Comb signifies need to organize your thoughts. Gypsies believe that if you are combing your heat in your dream foretells invitation to good friends.

Comedian symbolizes you to be more carefree.

Comet signifies you to free yourself from emotional and physical burdens.

Communion symbolizes a conflict between material and spiritual world.

Compact disk denotes opportunities.

Compass is the way to subconscious mind to show us the right way.

Completion signifies need for compliments.

Composer symbolizes new creative energies.

Computer symbolizes information and modern life.

Concentration Camp signifies fears from differences. If you have been in a concentration camp, it may signify a situation in your waking life witch is a memory of similar feeling at the time of concentration camp.

Concern-If you are concern in your dream signifies to pay attention for the concern.

Concert represents harmony and uplift of your spirit.

Concussion-Don't wait things to be happen-do something yourself.

Condom represents sexual possibilities, unwrapped condom symbolizes sexual frustration.

Conductor signifies abilities direct toward higher awareness.

Cong is a symbolic of ideas and feelings.

Confession—Are you feeling guilty of something?

Confetti signifies energies and success.

Confusing some element is confusing to you-try to analyze the symbol.

Constellation signifies mental process

Contact lens suggests paying closer attention before acting.

Contract signifies a commitment for a relationship or a project.

Convent signifies need for spiritual support.

Conversation represents your adaptability to situations in life.

Convict some situation makes you feel restricted.

Cookies signifies minor disputer annoy you.

Cooking signifies your need to be loved and want others to be depended on you and your desire to influence others.

Copper signifies power of healing (fang sue)

Coral signifies happiness and purification.

Cord signifies lack of independence.

Cork represents your adaptability in different situations.

Corn is a symbolic of growth and fertility.

Corn coda represents abundance.

Corridor is seen a passage from one phase in your life to other phase, represents soul circulation.

Corset—Are you feeling limited?

Costume-You are not really honest with other people around you.

Couch symbolizes relaxation or boredom.

Coughing signifies need to have more distance between yourself and others.

Counselor symbolizes your seeking kind of support or direction in your life.

Country side represents need to live simply and to relax, because your daily life is lacking of freedom.

Cousins represent your need to develop your character, kind of character that is already familiar to you.

Cow is a symbolic of fertility and motherhood.

Cowboy represents masculinity and your animalistic side.

Crack-Do you feel difficulties to keep your composure together.

Cradle represents depended relationship.

Crane symbolizes material love; you also like to give to your dearest ones.

Crater symbolizes past memories.

Crayons symbolize creativity.

Crazy-You are no longer depend of somebody.

Cream symbolizes richness.

Caricatures-Your life is bringing up your fears.

Credit cards symbolize work and money, if somebody is steeling your credit cars signifies that somebody is steeling your energy.

Cremation symbolizes purification.

Crescent symbolizes changes.

Crickets-Are you seeking guidance for some problem?

Crime-You are feeling quit and shame of something.

Crocodile forewarns from hidden fears, also signifies disappointments in love and false friendship.

Crop is a symbolic of self-love.

Cross symbolizes martyrdom or sacrifice, what is causing you to suffer?

Crossbones foretell danger.

Crossword signifies facing with a mental challenge.

Crowd signifies your need to have more space around you.

Crown is a symbolic of success.

Crucifix signifies new life.

Crucify-Why you are punishing yourself?

Cruel signifies that you are recognizing your negative aspects of your self.

Crush-You are under a stress over a decision you have to make.

Crystal symbolizes wholeness and healing.

Cuckoo symbolizes ticking and fate. Many people believe that as many times you hear cuckoo is calling that many years you still have time to live.

Cucumber is connected to sex and also signifies recovery.

Cult-Are you in some manipulating relationship?
Cultivate signifies your need to clear your thoughts.
Cup signifies healing.
Cupboard-You are revealing a secret.
Carry symbolizes your sensitive emotions.
Curse refers your inner fears.
Curtains signify secrecy and repression of thoughts.
Cut signifies imbalance, cutting symbolizes broken relationship.
Cymbals signify making noise from nothing.
Cypress symbolizes death and mourning.

D

Daffodil symbolizes inner growth.
D-If you are attacked by dagger forewarns of physical injury from an enemy.
Dahlias signify good luck in business.
Dairy symbolizes good fortune.
Daisy signifies freshness and innocence.
Dam-Are you overwhelmed with emotions?
Damask Rose foretells of wedding in the family.
Damson signifies richness.
Dance represents freedom and co-operation with yourself. If you are going to dance indicates happiness and celebration.
Dandelion signifies happy times with your lover.
Dandruff signifies lack of self-esteem.
Danger signifies difficulties in business.
Darkness signifies failure in the work, if you are lost in the darkness indicates that you have sufficient information to make a clear decision.
Dark board signifies you to express you anger more directly.
Darts-Did you say something harmful to somebody?
Date-To dream of a date signifies happy occasions in short time. If you are eating dates signifies you to be unhappy in your life.

Daughter signifies your famine aspect of yourself; the dream can be connected to your relationship with your daughter.

Dawn signifies rejuvenation.

Day-Try to remember what kind of day you have noticed, sunny day signifies success, cloudy day signifies sadness.

Deaf-Are you closing yourself of new experiences?

Death-Are you influenced by negative people, death signifies material loss. If you dreamt of a person who is already death-may signify a message to you.

If you dreamt of your own death indicates a transformable phase in your life. If you see someone death-what makes that person so special that the loved one embodies.

Dept signifies worries.

Decapitation signifies that you are not able to see the truth.

Decay signifies to forget the old situation before rebirth can happen.

December symbolizes wealth.

Decal signifies need to be more aware from your surroundings.

Deer symbolizes gentleness, female aspect with you.

Defecate-If you are being defecated on you maybe suffering from low self-esteem.

Delight signifies positive turn of events.

Demeter-You know how to support your dependence.

Demotion signifies that you are you out of control for some reason?

Demons—Negative forces indicate ultimate helplessness.

Den symbolizes efficiency.

Dentist signifies you being choked by scandal near you.

Depression-You are not able to see the causes of your problems.

Derrick-You are in your way to success.

Dessert represents celebration or temptation.

Destruction signifies chaos in your life.

Detective signifies the danger of an aspect within you. If you are a detective in your dream-you are seeking your hidden talents.

Detergent signifies need to clean up your image and attitude.

Determination represents ambition.

Devil signifies negative aspect of you. Also if you have being friendly with the devil signifies dealing with issues of morality.

Devotion serves as a reminder that nothing will be gained by deceit.

Dew symbolizes experiencing sense of refreshment.

Diamonds-If you see diamonds in your dream signifies wholeness of the self. Diamonds have been long time in the earth and they have got the perfect form, so they signify your brilliant consciousness. Gypsies believe that diamonds bring good fortune.

Diarrhea signifies some part of your life is going out of control.

Dictator-Usually the dictator signifies over controlling father.

Die is a symbolic of transformation, metaphorically dying can be dying of old habits.

Alternatively represents behaviors and feeling of depressed in your waking life.

Dead-If you dream that somebody is dead in your dream, the dream can happen and the message is given in advance only to survive from the shock, put usually dead symbolizes that feeling to that person are dead.

Diet indicates self control and a punishment to your self.

Difficulty symbolizes temporally illness.

Digging symbolizes hard work.

Dining room represents your knowledge and understanding.

Dinner—You need serious thinking with direction in your life. To eat dinner with others symbolizes your behaving in your social life.

Dinosaur signifies outdated attitudes.

Diploma symbolizes recognition for your work you have done.

Dirty symbolizes feeling of unworthy.

Disability signifies lowered self-esteem.

Disappear-Have you lost some aspect of yourself?

Disappointment-If you had a disappointment in your real life-your dream is a reflect.

Disaster-Are you afraid from changes?

Discovery signifies new times or personal development.

Disease-Sometimes the dreams foretell us of the illness before you are aware of the symptoms.

Disgrace symbolizes low moral.

Disguise-Are you hiding something in your waking life?

Dislike-You are not trying to be yourself, you are acting around you, playing some kind of role.

Dishes represent your attitudes. To wash dishes signifies new plans. To polish dishes signifies your trying to impress someone Broken dishes signifies lack of feelings.

Disinherited forewarn to re-evaluate your business plans.

Diskette-Have you given your ideas to others?

Disown signifies need to change your life right now!

Dispute signifies to dispute some aspects of you.

Distress is a symbolic of better future after long lasting disappointments.

Ditch signifies an embarrassing situation.

Divorce-Fear of separation, need to re organize your personal life.

Dizzy is a symbolic of contusion.

DNA-You have to learn from your past that you can move ahead in your life.

Doctor is a symbolic of healing.

Dog symbolizes protection, alternatively signifies that you don't trust people around you.

Dolls may serve as means of act out your wishes.

Dollhouse symbolizes your idealistic notions of family life.

Dolphins are symbolic of intellect and emotional trust, communication between conscious and unconscious aspects of you.

Dome signifies honor that will be bestowed upon you.

Donkey symbolizes hard work, also your stubbornness personality.

Door signifies new opportunities if the door is open signify your willingness to accept new ides. If you are locking the door you are closing yourself from others.

Doorbell signifies to you having new experiences.

Dormitory signifies realizing the value of education.

Doves symbolize peace and harmony. Traditionally a dove symbolizes a message.

Down-Maybe you have made a wrong decision?

Drafted-Do you feel pressure from some people around you?

Dragon symbolizes good fortune and sexual power. Traditionally a dragon symbolizes efforts of wizard and willingness to wholeness.

Destroy signifies to destroy the evil.

Dragonfly symbolizes the changes.

Drain indicates external force is affecting a situation in your life.

Drama-If you are writing a drama denotes that you will find yourself submerged in dept. To see drama signifies reunited with old friends.

Drawers represent your inner state of mind.

Drawing signifies creative, your artist talents.

Dream signifies your emotional state-you are worried about a situation you are going through.

Dress represents a famine outlook.

Drill indicates new experiences.

Drinking represents spiritual refreshment. If you are drinking alcohol, you are seeking escape. If you are drinking vine symbolizes diving power.

Dripping-Are you experiencing something disturbing witch is affecting your psyche?

Driving License signifies your identity crises.

Driving signifies your life journey and how you are navigating through life, just notice the way how you are driving.

If it is a mountain road what higher you clamp in life that harder it is to stay at the top.

Dromedary foretells unexpected honor.

Drop-It may present your carelessness-you don't care of somebody or some idea is not important to you.

Drowning signifies that you overwhelmed by emotions. If somebody is drowning symbolizes that you are involved with something that is beyond your control.

Drugs-For what do you need drugs?

Drums signify strong will. To hear drums represents the rhythm of life.

Drunk-Are you acting careless?

Dryer-Maybe you need to dry old feelings?

Duck-Flying duck represents spiritual freedom. Maybe you have done a mistake and it is difficult to put the things in order again. Also the ducks are multitalented, they can fly, swim and walk-so they represent your flexibility.

Duel-The positive and negative aspects of you are not in balance.

Dulcimer signifies carefree attitudes.

Dump-It is hard to find company to persuade your point of view.

Dummy-Some relationship makes you empty.

Dungeon-With your experience you will manage to overcame in your life.

Dunghill signifies fortune.

Dusk-Gloomy outlook is your endeavors. Maybe you also feel neglected.

Dwarf-In tales dwarfs are diligent so it is a positive dream, because you will get your goals.

Dwarf signifies your need to be more connected to the nature and to the earth.

Dye-It depends what colors you are using, bright colors signify vitality, black and brown colors usually signify depression and white purity.

E

Eagerness is an optimistic dream, do you have new ideas?

Eagles symbolize freedom. Also renewal of high desires. If you eat eagle flesh in your dream signifies help from very powerful person.

Ears signify bad news.

Earrings-Please pay attention what others have to say you. Also earrings symbolize desire of affection.

Earth signifies sense of being grounded.

Earthquake-Your foundations are shaking up, earthquake symbolizes helplessness.

Earning symbolizes unpleasant news.

East-Sunrise starts from east and east symbolizes spiritual enlightenment and creation.

Easter is a symbolic of Christianity and signifies spiritual rebirth.

Easter egg symbolizes unusual wonder.

Eating signifies loneliness and cut off from social ties. If you are eating with company signifies personal gain.

Echo signifies need to repeat yourself that others can trust your power of worlds.

Eclipse indicates self-doubt.

Ecstasy symbolizes joy and happiness.

Education signifies desire of knowledge.

EEL-Do you have issues with commitments?

Eggs are symbolic of birth and fertility signifies that new ideas are coming. To see a nest with eggs represent financial gain.

Egypt signifies the roots of your emotions.

Ejaculation signifies lost of control. Do you need more space?

Elderberries symbolize comfort.

Elderly represents wisdom.

Election signifies your need to affect others.

Electricity is a symbolic of life energy.

Elephant is a symbolic of power, if you are ridding an elephant indicates that you are in control of unconscious.

Elevator represents ups and downs in your life.

Elf symbolizes disharmony in your life.

Elk indicates that you need to take more care of your health.

Eloquent symbolizes pleasant news (if you give the speed).

E-mail signifies your need to reach out to people.

Embankment signifies that you have struggle for higher status.

Embarrassment symbolizes hidden weakness.

Embrace signifies of an unwelcome quest.

Embroidery signifies an ability to do everything in a best possible way.

Embryo is a very common dream. If you really are pregnant, it may refer to your feelings of need to be protected.

Emerald is a gemstone that represents growth and durability, also entering healing stages.

Emotionless-Are you neglecting your own feelings?

Emotions signifies to act out your feelings which normally would not been expressed.

Emperor represents completion and creativity.

Employment signifies to put more focus on your personal life.

Empress-You will be honored highly for a reason that you already know.

Emptiness—Something is missing in your life.

Enchantment indicates that you are being manipulated.

Enchantress symbolizes famine power.

Enclosure represents limitation.

Encyclopedia signifies need to enrich your mind.

End signifies the goals that have been reached.

Enemy represents a resolution to some inner conflict or problem in your waking life.

Engagement-Maybe you are too much lonely and your dream tries to resolve your loneliness.

Engineer indicates evaluating a situation and. how various pieces fit together.

Entrails symbolize misery and despair.

Envelope signifies new opportunities, unopened envelope symbolizes sad news.

Epicure signifies your desire to cultivate your taste to highest potential.

Epidemic signifies worries of individual tasks.

Epilepsy-You need to express more your emotions.

Equator indicates to search for balance with you.

Eraser signifies need to clear up some mistakes.

Erection symbolizes your creative power and energy.

Errands signify your mutual understanding.

Eruption-Maybe you are experiencing an upheaval in your life.

Escalator indicates moment between various levels of consciousness.

Escape—You are really not facing problems that aren't going away.

Estate signifies your inheritance.

Eucalyptus represents protection or need to be protected.

Evacuation-Why you are isolating yourself and don't want to show your emotions?

Evaporation signifies a positive transformation.

Eve is a sexual dream.

Evening is a symbolic of unrealized hopes.

Evening gown signifies social pleasures.

Eviction-Some situation makes you hopeless.

Evil is a forbidden or hidden aspect of you.

Ex-It is usually in your current life that brings you feelings of same emotions from your past relationship.

Exam signifies your fears and failures.

Exchange signifies a profitable gain.

Execution-Maybe you suffer misfortune from carelessness of others-or maybe you saw a movie with execution?

F

Fable-If you are in a fable, represents need to face the reality.

Face-The face you see in your dream is your chosen persona-usually as oppose to real you.

Faceless-Need to find out who you really are, you are seeking for real you.

Facelift signifies need for new self-image.

Factory is a symbolic of unchanging habits.

Failure signifies fears in ability to confront some unconscious feelings.

Faithless foretells of happy marriage.

Fakir-Phenomenal changes in your life.

Falcon signifies need to be focused to your goals.

Fall is a very typical dream, indicates lack of control and lack of support in your waking life. Free falling through water signifies that you are overwhelmed with feelings-it is a natural way to release emotions in the dream.

Fame signifies unrealized disappointments.

Famine-It is not a good sign, represents negative turn in business and health.

Family represents warmth and love; try to remember who you specially noticed in your dream.

Fan-If you are funning yourself in your dream, represents lack of self-confidence.

Fangs-Have you hurt someone with bad worlds?

Farewell forewarns of unpleasant news.

Farm represents growth and vitality.

Farmer signifies need to work hard in order for benefits.

Farming represents your need to express feelings more directly. Alternatively farmer represents your need to nature in order to get vitality.

Fasting represents self-renewal and self-cleansing.

Fat-Good luck will change your life, alternatively signifies fear of gaining weight.

Father is a symbolic of protection. If you dream that your
father is dead symbolizes need to be protected with caution in
conducting business. Gypsies believe that father's dead forewarns
of misfortune in the family, put if you dream from your father in
common foretells of love.
Father in law signifies happy occasions with your family.
Faucet signifies strong mind and self-control.
Fawn is a symbolic of faithfulness and love.
Fear-Sometimes you like to show yourself more successful to other
than you really are.
Feast foretells surprises in the near future.
Feather symbolizes comfort of the life, put also financial gains.
Feces signify releasing the negativity from your body and relax,
and then you can allow new emotions come to your life. According
to Freud feces symbolizes your anxiety.
Feet symbolize your foundations and stability. In India the feet are
holiest part of body and symbolize your independence.
Fence-If you are climbing to the top of fence foretells success. On
the other hand-do you feel fenced in, or need to shut off from the
entire world?
Fermentation symbolizes spiritual transformation.
Fergus symbolizes hopes.
Ferret-Are you unfaithful to others?
Ferry signifies your new ideas or goals.
Fertilizer refers to your growth.
Festival-Are you depended from others, even you don't want to.
Fetus-Something creative is happening to you.
Fever-You have fever because you don't want to express your
feelings.
Fiddle signifies harmony in the home.
Field-If the field is green signifies growth and freedom. If you see
in your dream dry field signifies pessimism.
Fig leaves signify loss of innocence.
Fighting is conflict between some aspects of yourself, if you fight
with someone you know signifies the conflict between the person
and you. Gypsies believe that if you have a fight with someone
signifies your success with your plans, put if the fight is in the
business field signifies a loss.

Figs-Is a positive sing, if you eat figs signifies good health and if the figs are growing signifies a profit and wealth. Fig is also a sexual symbolic.

Figure-To see strange figures in your dream symbolizes a mental distress.

File symbolizes unfavorable events which will be a source of much anxiety.

Filer signifies need to smooth out edges of relationship with someone or of your own personality.

Film signifies analyzing yourself.

Find-You are recognizing a part of yourself that has been undeveloped.

Fingers are a symbolic of non-verbal communications and mental dexterity. Gypsies believe that to see fingers in your dream signifies a bad fight.

Fingernails represent glamour put if the nails are growing rapidly signifies your desire to reach to something.

Fire is a symbolic of transformation and enlighten. Something new is coming to your life. If the fire is under control it is a metaphor for inner transformation.

Fire-engine-Do you overlook your own needs, use more distraction.

Fire band symbolizes good fortune.

Fired-If you are fired from your work in your dream indicates that you want to end some situation.

Firefly signifies great ideas are coming from you to daylight.

Fireplace symbolizes comfort. If you see fire from fireplace symbolizes burning desire.

Fireworks symbolize creativity and great talents

Fish is the symbol of Christianity and signifies good luck and nourishment. If a woman gets a fish signifies a pregnancy and boy child.

Fish market signifies joy and pleasures.

Fisherman-What do you try to catch in your waking life?

Fishing-If you are fishing in your dream signifies confronting difficult emotions from your unconscious, put it is good to do it, fishing is a natural way to calm emotions.

Fist symbolizes power and aggression.

Fits symbolizes loss of employment.

Fix signifies need to re-evaluate some relationship in your waking life

Flag symbolizes your duty to country and patriotism.

Flame symbolizes need to invest your best efforts to get success.

Flamingo indicates new experiences.

Flashlight signifies your ability to find the way out in situation

Fleas signify a manipulated relationship by someone near you.

Fleet symbolize sudden change in business,

Fleur De Liz is a symbolic of a spiritual power.

Flight signifies your feeling to be limited, you need more freedom and space around you.

Flirting signifies serious relationship in the near future.

Floating- "Your worries will go with the flow" and new energies will flow to you.

Flood signifies that your emotions are overwhelming you.

Floor represents the division between your unconscious and conscious mind.

Flour symbolizes our basic needs to manage in everyday life.

Flower is a symbolic of beauty and gain. Red flowers symbolize love and white flowers purity and sadness.

Flute-To listen flute music signifies harmony in your life.

Flying signifies sense of freedom and rebuilds your energies. Flying to unknown places signifies flying away from hard reality. Traditionally flying signifies a long journey, if you have a successful landing symbolizes graduation from great work you have done. Flying also signifies high level of ambitions, duties and success.

Fly Trap symbolizes some kind of malicious plan set forth against you.

Foal symbolizes new energies.

Food represents physical and emotional nourishment and also new energies. Fruits are a symbolic of sensuality, frozen food imply gold emotions, stale food need to revitalizes.

Foot is a symbolic of lack of freedom or maybe you have chosen a wrong way.

Footprints symbolize a heritance.

Forehead signifies good judgment and fairness.

Foreign language signifies a message from your unconscious that you don't yet understand.

Foreigner symbolizes unfamiliar aspect of you.

Forest-If you are lost in the forest you are seeking for better understanding. Forest symbolizes our unconscious.

Forgetting-Maybe you really have forgotten something.

Fork-If you see somebody eating with the fork represents worries that will be solved with the help of a good friend.

Formaldehyde-Please release old emotions.

Fort symbolizes constantly defending yourself.

Fortress is a symbolic of healing.

Fortune telling signifies your fears of the future.

Fossils symbolize death.

Found represents a contact with some aspect of your psyche or unconscious. Found signifies also to new direction.

Foundation signifies that you are well-prepared for any situation before you

Fountain represents new relationship.

Fowl symbolizes temporary worries.

Fox-Clever as a fox, you know how to solve problems.

Frames symbolize limitations

Fraud signifies need to re-new yourself.

Freckles symbolize lost love.

Freeway is a symbolic of liberty and freedom.

French symbolize love and romantic.

Friend-Friends will bring you good news and happy tidings.

Frisbee signifies lack of completion.

Frog symbolizes unexpected; you are taking steps towards some goal. To hear sound of frogs signifies unpleasant visit. Fengsue represents a frog as a symbolic of good luck.

Frosting symbolizes hard work put also new opportunities.

Fruit symbolizes growth and financial gains and of course sexuality.

Frustration represents concerns that your life is not going in the direction you want.

Funeral symbolizes ending to the situation. If you are in funeral of somebody else you are burying an old relationship. If you dream burying of your still living parents signifies you desire to get your own independence, the death of parents is only symbolic death.

Fungus represents negative emotions.

Furnace symbolizes power and energy.

Furniture signifies your relationship with others and how they fit into your life.

Furs are symbolic of your animistic nature.

Future signifies your hopes of how the things will turn out

G

Gad-It is better to be silent, even if you thing different way.

Galaxy signifies your awareness to creativity.

Gale-Don't loose your control, you will find solutions to your problems.

Gall Bladder-Don't let your bitterness to grow out.

Gallows-If you see gallows in your dream symbolizes bad luck.

Gambling signifies you not taking responsibility for your decisions.

Game-If you are killing an animal in your dream represents your ability to keep your animalistic nature in control.

Games represent relaxation

Gangrene foretells of loss and death.

Gap signifies that something is lacking in your idea.

Garage-Do you feel yourself without any direction in your life?

Garbage-If you are throwing away your garbage signifies throwing your negative habits away.

Garden is a symbolic of stability and inner growth.

Garland represents completeness.

Garlic is a symbolic of health and profitable business.

Garnet is a gemstone that symbolizes loyalty and love.

Garret signifies your increasing finances.

Garter signifies titillation.

Gas signifies that you have to re-energize yourself. Gypsies believe tat gas forewarns of scandals.

Gate represents new opportunities and possibilities.

Gauze signifies that you have some problems with your health.

Gavel symbolizes justice.

Gazelle symbolizes your soul lighten up.

Gear represents a new direction in your life.

Gecko is a symbolic of agreement.

Geese symbolizes that you are well crowned.

Geisha is a symbolic of beauty and grace.

Gems are a symbolic of love and happiness.

Genie symbolizes creative.

Genitals signify issues of pleasure.

Geography foretells of traveling in near future.

Geranium is a symbolic of elegance.

Germs symbolize lack of motivation.

Geyser symbolizes an outburst of emotion.

Ghost signifies aspects of yourself, you can't control painful thoughts.

Ghoul-Your negative ways are disturbing your growth.

Giant is a symbolic of an issue that is dominating you.

Gift indicates that you are being rewarded or recognized for your giving nature.

Gig represents freedom.

Ginger is a symbolic of confront in your life.

Ginseng represents virility.

Giraffe—symbolizes to take a boarder view on your life and where it is headed.

Girdle-You are hiding your real nature to please others.

Girlfriend represents your relationship and feelings.

Girls are a symbolic of innocent nature.

Giving-If something is giving to you; suggest need to appreciate the gifts you have.

Glacier represents golf emotions.

Gladiolas are symbolic of joy and happiness.

Glass-If you are looking through glass represents your openness. If the glass is broken symbolizes a change in your life

Glass Blower symbolizes that you can't emplaning a change for better future.

Glass House represents that you are being watched.

Glass Slipper is a symbolic of transformation.

Gleaners signify prosperity in business.

Glider symbolizes that the things are breeze for you.

Gleaners signify prosperity in business.

Globe signifies complete control in your life.

Gloomy indicates that you need more clarity to understand some problem.

Gloves symbolize your need to express your creative side, if you take gloves off symbolizes respect.

Glow symbolizes enlightenment.

Glue symbolizes some situation and you don't know how to get out from it.

Goal symbolizes success.

Goalie symbolizes your capabilities.

Goat signifies lack of judgment, it is also a warning that somebody wants to know your business plans.

Goblet symbolizes the famine aspect of you.

God symbolizes the notion of perfection and your spiritual expression. If God speaks with you signifies that you have guilty feelings and you are afraid from punishment.

Godzilla-Do you feel out of control for some reason?

Goggles signify that you are trying to protect yourself from emotional harm.

Gold-If you find gold in your dream you are discovered something valuable about yourself.

Goldfish symbolizes money and success.

Gold Leaves foretell wealth and good times ahead.

Golf symbolizes individual accomplishment and you will have success.

Gondola signifies to romance.

Gong symbolizes end to some situation-or new start.

Goose symbolizes fertility and motherly love.

Goosebumps symbolizes frigid attitudes.

Gooseberries-Your problems will turn to happiness.

Gopher signifies need to take action, because you have been manipulated.

Gorilla-To see gorilla in your dream signifies your primitive impulses and over acting.

Gossip indicates that you are using others to get information without any accurate.

Gourd represents abundance.

Gout signifies minor financial loss.

Government signifies power and large reflect of society.

Grade represents how well you have studied in your life lessons, experience and understanding.

Graduation signifies successful transition to higher level of ability.

Grafting signifies to your successful connections.

Grain is a symbolic of wealth and happiness.

Grammar signifies difficulties with your communication.

Grandchild represents renewal of life and innocence and purity.

Grandmother is a symbolic of unconditional love; she might have some message to you or your family.

Grandparents symbolize love, security and wisdom.

Grapefruit is a symbolic of freshness, state of mind and fruits of your labor.

Grapes-If you are picking grapes signify your realization of your desires and also signify to wealth.

Grass is a symbolic of natural protection.

Grasshopper symbolizes freedom or spiritual enlightenment.

Grave signifies something that has completed in your life. Gypsies believe that if you are standing beside an open grave signifies that your friend is deceiving you and grave signifies to serious difficulties.

Graveyard represents discarded aspects of you.

Grease signifies need to get your life straighten out.

Greek signifies acceptance of your ideas.

Greenhouse represents transformation.

Greeting Card is a symbolic of surprises.

Griffon represents physical strength; positive aspects of change.

Grim Reaper is a symbolic of negative aspect of you.

Grins-Try to avoid need of others and try to thing how you can manage to arrange the things alone.

Groans-Enemies have time to underling you if you don't decide quickly.

Groceries symbolize comfort.

Groom-If you a female signifies your will to marry, for a male it is a commitment for a relationship.

Grotto signifies to the end of relationship.

Ground represents your foundation; it is a boundary between your conscious and unconscious.

Grout signifies need to piece together a situation.

Growing symbolizes spiritual enlightenment.

Guard represents rational thinking.

Guardian signifies that you are treated with consideration by your friend.

Guest is a symbolic of interests in your life. If you are a quest signifies temporally problem in your life.

Guide-Higher forces are guiding you toward your goals.

Guillotine signifies eruption of strong emotions and anger; need to think twice before you act.

Guilt signifies to your failures and negative feelings that you have.

Guinea Pig-You will learn from your mistakes.

Guitar represents passion and emotions.

Gulls signify relationship with logic and unconscious; dead gulls signify separation from friends.

Gum symbolizes sticky situation that you have to solve by yourself.

Gun-To hears gun shutting signify to negative emotions. If someone is shutting you with a gun represent some confrontation in your waking life.

Guru suggests your trying to be more powerful in the world.

Guts represent strength and stamina.

Gutter symbolizes unhappiness to others.

Gymnast signifies grace.

Gypsy signifies your desire to look towards to future.

H

Hag represents nurturance.

Haggard-If you see your own face grown haggard you may be under huge emotional stress.

Hail-You may be shut down emotionally?

Hair signifies sexual virility. How is the condition of your hair; if it is tangled, it may represent confusion in your life and if you have a haircut signifies ambitions? Long hair signifies difficulties to make decisions. Strong and shiny hair signifies vitality.

Gypsies believe that if you are combing (brushing) your hair in your dreams, good friend will invite you for a party, put if you are loosing your hair signifies sorrow.

Haircut-Do you feel criticized unfairly?

Hairdresser-If you are at a hairdresser signifies that you are ready to move a different attention.

Half indicates that something in your waking life is unsolved. On the other hand signifies need to open a compromise.

Hallways signify to physical or emotional passages in your life.

Halloween signifies death and the under world.

Hallucination represents repressed emotions. Alternatively are you trying to hide something?

Halo is a symbolic of perfectionist.

Ham signifies desire for attention.

Hamburger signifies experiences and need to learn from them.

Hammer signifies masculine attitudes. It is also a symbolic of inner battles.

Hamper signifies negative feelings.

Hamster-Are you able to separate sex and love?

Hand is a symbolic of communications. If you hold hand with someone signifies a relationship; what kind of hand, cold or warm signifies your feelings to that relationship. If you hand is injured in your dream denotes an attack to your ego and if you see blood on your hand signifies guilty feelings. If you wash your hand in the dream signifies that you are not willing to take any responsibly in something. If you see only a hand in your dream signifies support to your new idea. Hand of God keeps you alive in difficult times.

Handcuffs signify that new opportunities are shut off to you.

Handicap signifies weakness.

Handkerchiefs-If you are waving good-bye with the handkerchiefs signifies social downfall.

Handle signifies your need to handle the life.

Handshake symbolizes new beginning-or end to some situation.

Handwriting signifies your creativity.

Hanger signifies need for more motivation.

Happy signifies your try to compensate for sadness in your waking life.

Harbor signifies separation from stormy relationship and refills your energies.

Hare signifies transformation.

Harem is a sexual dream.

Harmonica symbolizes your need for happiness in your waking life.

Harness symbolizes lack of freedom.

Harp is a symbolic for healing.

Harvesting signifies your need still to develop your career and goals.

Hat signifies role you are playing.

Hate signifies your fear of confrontations.

Haunted signifies unpleasant memories.

Hawaii signifies need for some relaxation.

Hank denotes suspicions are curling around you

Hay denotes that nothing comes easily in life.

Head signifies wisdom and understanding.

Headache signifies that you really can have a headache in your waking life. Alternatively signifies to keep your emotions in control.

Headphone indicates that you are in tune with your emotions.

Healing signifies the need for emotional healing.

Hear-Is it true that nobody is paying any attention to what you are saying?

Hearse symbolizes a new beginning.

Heart signifies the truth and love.

Heart attack signifies lack of support.

Hearth signifies family values.

Heater signifies comfort.

Heaven signifies optimism and hopes.

Heavy symbolizes you responsibilities.

Hedge symbolizes restrictions.

Heel signifies vulnerability.

Height signifies that you have reached your goal.

Helicopter is symbolic of ambition and achievements.

Hell signifies your inner fears and guilty feelings.

Helmet-Keep your thoughts closely guarded.

Help-If you help someone signifies your talent to active a goal and willingness to compromise your beliefs. If you need help signifies loss or you are overwhelmed.

Hen symbolizes gossip.

Herbs signifies your need to approach towards to relationship; try to look the situation different way.

Hercules signifies need for individual freedom.

Herd-Try to make your own decisions; don't follow others.

Hermaphrodite represents balance.

Hermit signifies need to be alone.

Hero signifies your inner straight or weakness.

Heron-You will active much success through your efforts.

Herpes-Maybe you have practiced unsafe sex and are expressing your regrets.

Hex-If somebody is putting a hex on you symbolizes hurtful feelings.

Hexagram represents harmony between spiritual and physical.

Hickey-Are you acting too much with emotions instead of thinking things out more clearly?

H-Are you withholding some information. It may also represent feeling of quilt, if you are hiding of some author.

Hieroglyphics denotes that you will have many obstacles as you try to find your truth.

High School represents need to start to prepare to real life.

Highway represents sense of direction of your life, straight highway signifies piece and harmony, bumpy road reflects emotional disharmony.

Hiking symbolizes strong will.

Hill-If you are standing on top of the hill signifies that you have success with your targets. If you are climbing a hill symbolizes struggles you still have.

Hippie is a symbolic of freedom.

Hippopotamus signifies power.

Hips-It relates to getting things done.

History-Are you trying to relive past emotions?

Hit-Don't keep negative emotions inside you.

Hitchhiking signifies that you are getting more that you suppose to earn.

Hives signify fears.

Hockey-You need full emotions with your way to live.

Hoe signifies that you are ready to growth after few hard battles.

Hog signifies that you don't like to share your emotions with others.

Hole-Are you feeling empty inside, you need new interest in your life.

Holidays-If you dream of holidays, it seems to have time for rest and new interest to your life.

Hollow symbolizes hidden secrets.

Holly represents memories of family.

Hologram symbolizes your notions of perfection.

Home- "home, sweet home" there are your basic, needs and values. If you dream of your childhood home signifies your willingness to build your own family.

Homeless signifies of your unsure ness.

Homosexual signifies to self love.

Honey represents piece and happiness.

Hoof signifies to your material gain.

Hoop-To dream of a hoop in your dream signifies that you are covering from a person.

Horizon symbolizes future plans.

Horn-To dream of horns of animal represents conflict.

Hornets symbolize danger.

Horse is a symbolic of vitality. If you see a black horse in your dream signifies mystery and unknown and if you see a white horse signifies good fortune and purity.

If you see herd of wild horses signifies to uncontrolled emotions.

If you are riding a horse signifies success and if the horse is out of control signifies that you are carried away with your passions.

Horserace symbolizes your sexual energy.

Horseradish-Are you offend others without knowing it?

Horseshoe is a symbolic of good fortune.

Hose symbolizes renewal.

Hospital signifies your need to improve your physical or mental health.

Hospitality-You do things and help others without waiting any return.

Hospitality represents your feelings in your waking life.

Hot-If you are hot in your dream signifies to passion and emotion.

Hot Pepper symbolizes your hot temper.

Hot Tub symbolizes your unveiling aspects of your unconscious.
Hotel signifies temporally escape from everyday life.
Hour refers to passage of time.
House represents your soul and self. Rooms in the house indicate
a specific aspect of your psyche and the basement signifies
unconscious. If you see a new house in your dream signifies new
experiences.
Howling symbolizes wounded emotions.
Hugging symbolizes your caring nature.
Humid suggest being lacking of understanding in some situation.
Hummingbird-Small ideas may posses much potential.
Hunting signifies need to fulfill some inner desires. If you kill an
animal signifies to repress or destroy in instinctive past of you.
Hurdle signifies the barriers that you have in your life.
Hurricane signifies unexpected changes occurring in your life.
Hurry signifies lack of planning for a situation.
Husband signifies your relationship and feelings in your waking
life.
Hug represents comfort.
Hyacinth symbolizes jealousy.
Hydrant symbolizes renewal and rejuvenation.
Hyena—Are you overwhelmed with relationship?
Hypnotize signifies troubles.
Hysterectomy-You are going into new state of growth in your life.

I

Ibis symbolizes aspirations.
Ice-You are feeling rigid-let your feelings to be known.
Ice Cream denotes pleasure and satisfaction in your waking life.
Ice Skating-You need to trust yourself more.
Icicles-If the icicles are melting in your dream-you are overcoming
your problems-oppose if the icicles are forming symbolizes
troubles.

Ideal-To dream of ideas symbolizes utmost honesty in any case that you are involved in the idea.

Identification signifies your own self-confidence.

Idiot signifies that your thoughts are lacing of clarity.

Idle-Now it is time to take action, only thing what you really want to do.

Idols-You are worshipping false valves.

Igloo-You will meet someone that appears frigid on the outside, put it is a really caring person on inside.

Ignore-It may reflect your real experiences of being ignored by that person.

Iguana-It is a symbolic of good luck. Alternatively may represent your different aspects in different situations.

Illness denotes unpleasant changes; on the other hand pay attention to the areas of body that you feel yourself ill.

Illumining foretells failure.

Imitation is the best form of flattery. If you are imitating others-you may try to imitate the wisdom of that person.

Immortal signifies that you are afraid of some changes.

IPM signifies chaos.

Impale-You are set free symbolically from physical limitations of your own psyche.

Impeach-You are not afraid in letting others know who you rally are.

Implements-To see broken implement in your dream denotes failure in business and as well in private life.

Impotence denotes a fear of loosing power.

Inauguration denotes rise in your current status.

Incense denotes a good level of awareness.

Incest signifies erotic desires and also famine and masculine aspects of you.

Incoherent symbolizes high level of excitement.

Income signifies financial worries.

Incubator signifies fresh, new ideas.

Independent signifies a rival who may do you wrong.

Indian is a symbolic of wisdom. Alternatively symbolizes the primitive and instinctual aspect of you.

Indigestion signifies gloomy surroundings; maybe also a situation that is really not for you.

Infection signifies negative ideas that you have internalized. Find out where you have an infection

Infidelity signifies that you are unsatisfied with your current relationship.

Infants symbolize surprises.

Infertile symbolizes lack of creativity.

Inheritance symbolizes success and opportunities.

Injection is a healing dream.

Injury symbolizes hard work and trying too much.

Ink represents creativity put if the ink is spilled on your finger symbolizes minor troubles.

In-law advises you to be more careful.

Inn signifies pleasures if the inn is well-furnished and oppose signifies unhappy journeys.

Insanity represents your retreat from reality.

Inscription symbolizes a message from your unconscious.

Insect signifies you to organize your thoughts.

Insurance refers to lack of trust.

Intercom-If you hear a voice from intercom represents a message from your unconscious; you have realizes solution to a problem.

Intermarriage symbolizes trouble and loss.

Internet signifies need for communication.

Interrupt-Sometimes the things are not like you want them to be

Interview-If you see yourself in a interview denotes your anxiety over being judges by others.

Intoxicated-Some situation makes you mad.

Intruder symbolizes unwanted sexual attention.

Inventor—You may be trying to identify a higher level of consciousness

Invisible-Are you trying to withdraw from the realities of the life?

Invitation foretells happiness that is coming.

Iris is a symbolic of wisdom and faith.

Iron signifies strength and will-power.

Ironing signifies orderliness.

Island signifies relaxation and comfort.

Ivory symbolizes purity.

Ivy foretells good luck ahead.

J

Jab-Don't doubt about abilities.

Jackal refers to manipulation.

Jack row signifies disputes and quarrels

Jacket represents the image that you want to represent to the outside world.

Jackhammer-You need huge changes in your life.

Jacuzzi signifies need to clean yourself from the negativity, especially from your sexual life.

Jade is a gemstone that represents the healing power and self-development.

Jaguar represents pleasure and power.

Jail signifies that your lover is unfaithful.

Jailer-You are being restraint in someway.

Jam-If you are making jam in your dream foretells happy family life.

Janitor forewarns of unfortunate in business.

January symbolizes love.

Jar signifies that your feelings are shaken for some reason.

Jasmine symbolizes short lived pleasures.

Jasper is a gemstone of healing and vitality.

Javelin-If you stabbed by a javelin signifies freedom.

Jaw signifies stubbornness.

Jaybird signifies hard work; put at least you enjoy of your doings.

Jealousy signifies your feelings from your waking life.

Jelly is a metaphor for something that at last is taking shape.

Jellyfish is a hidden aggression in some aspect of your waking life.

Jesus foretells that your greatest desires will be realized. If Jesus speaks with you in your dream signifies peace of mind.

Jet-ski-You are exposing aspects of your conscious in full force.

Jets forewarn unlucky in business.

Jewelry-What kind of jewelry do you see in your dream? If you see ruby signifies unconditional love, Safire represents good family life, emerald represents strong, everlasting relationship opal signifies need to know your own truth and diamonds signify

brilliant opportunities and love, onyx represents luck with business.
Gold signifies to your own sense of self-worth and personal valve.
Jewelry box represents your self-value.
Jewels—If you find jewels in your dream signifies rapid
advancement.
Job-If you are looking for a job; you may feel frustrated in your
current situation of your life.
Jockey foretells unexpected gift.
Jogging-Don't you want any changes in your life?
Joint represents flexibility.
Joke signifies your feeling of frustration.
Joshua tree represents strength and courage.
Journal symbolizes memories, put alternatively try to remember
what did you read?
Journey signifies self discovery and circumstances you may
experiencing.
Joy denotes harmony.
Judge denotes guilty feelings.
Jug-If the jugs are empty foretells of estrangement by friends due
to your conduct.
Broken mugs symbolize bad luck.
Juice represents vitality.
Jukebox signifies to try more to find better condition to your life.
July foretells good fortune.
Jumping signifies not to be afraid.
June signifies unusual gains.
Jungle signifies aspects of you.
Junk symbolizes your need to rid off old habits.
Junkyard represents frustration which you have kept inside.
Jupiter is a planet of security and justice.
Jury-Are you feeling that others are judging you?
Justice is a symbolic of false statements. If others demand justice
from you signifies your conducts are being questioned.

K

Kaleidoscope signifies diversity.

Kangaroo signifies aggression.

Karaoke signifies you to understand more potential that you have.

Karate signifies to you concentrate directly to your goals.

Keg-If the kegs are full signifies that you are in the right way to win your struggle and if the kegs are empty signifies you to find a different way.

Kelp symbolizes emotional difficulties.

Key- "The keys of luck" symbolizes opportunities to open new doors as well as secrets. Put if you loose a key signifies fear of loosing something important to you.

Keyhole signifies to curiosity put also suggest to find a better perspective on life.

Kick represents aggression that you are unable to express in your waking life. If you are kicking a ball signifies indicates time free of worries.

Kid symbolizes love and loving nature.

Kidnapper signifies need for more concentration to reach your goals.

Kidneys represent need for cleansing.

Killing-If you are killing someone in your dream signifies that you are loosing your self-control. (What kind of feelings you have to that person in your waking life?) If you have been killed in your dream refers to huge changes that are happening in your life.

Killer-If you are a killer in your dream signifies a healing process, because you like to finish a negative aspect of you.

King is a symbolic of control and power.

Kiss denotes love and harmony. If you see others kissing in your dreams; maybe you are involved too much in their life. To kiss a good friend represents your respect for your friend.

Kitchen represents transformation and spiritual nourishment.

Kite signifies that you are well-grounded with all your ambition.

Kitten symbolizes troubles.

Knapsack symbolizes secrets and responsibilities that you are caring.

Knee-Do you take too many responsibilities; you should share them with others.

Knife symbolizes anger and separation. To dream of dull knife denotes that you are working too hard for nothing.

Knitting signifies your creativity.

Knob signifies turning issues or conditions around you.

Knocker symbolizes opportunities, signifies also your seeking for spiritual guidance.

Knocking signifies a new opportunity will be offered to you.

Knuckles symbolize hard work.

Koala symbolizes security and protection.

Krishna symbolizes spiritual knowledge.

Kumquats signify good fortune.

L

Label denotes your need for order.

Labor-You will have success with hard work.

Laboratory signifies testing yourself

Labyrinth-If you are a labyrinth signifies troubles.

Lace signifies your sensuality, lace curtains foretells secrets.

Ladder-If you are climbing up a ladder suggest that you have reach higher awareness

And if you are climbing down a ladder signifies disappointments; if you are falling down from a ladder denotes failures or risks. To walk under a ladder signifies bad luck.

Ladle signifies love for children.

Ladybug symbolizes good fortune.

Lagoon denotes misunderstanding in your worlds.

Lake is a symbolic of state of mind; if the lake is clear symbolizes piece of mind and if the lake is disturbed denotes emotional problems.

Lamb represents innocent and purity.

Lame signifies failure.

Lament-First you have to struggle only then you can get pleasure.

Lamp signifies enlightenment and inspiration. Broken lamp is a symbolic of misfortune.

Lampshade indicates that you are trying to be noticeable.

Lanai signifies that you are receptive to new ides.

Lance is a symbolic of masculine power. If you can break a lance in your dream signifies your overcoming impossible task.

Land signifies need to be grounded.

Landlord refers to your rational and responsible side.

Landscape—According to Freud the landscape symbolizes human body.

My opinion is to consider what kind of elements you see in the landscape, and then you can understand your life and relationships.

Landslide symbolizes emotional overload.

Language-If you hear foreign language in your dream indicates a message from your unconscious that you will understand later on.

Lantern symbolizes good fortune

Lap-If you are holding someone on your lap denotes that you are open to comfortable criticism.

Lapis is a gemstone of accepting and deep understanding.

Lard symbolizes good fortune.

Lark-To hear a lark singing in your dreams symbolizes you to find happiness and luck with business.

Larva symbolizes transformation.

Laser symbolizes clarity and truth.

Lasso-If you are trying to lasso an animal foretells finding a real love.

Latch signifies that you'll receive an unwelcome appeal for help.

Late signifies that you are unready in your current situation to handle anything new.

Latin-If you hear Latin in your dream signifies that you will rise to a position of prominence.

Laughing signifies release of joy. If you hear children laughing foretells happiness and vitality.

Laundry-Need to clean your act; if you are in laundry with someone else foretells gossip.

Laurel symbolizes success.

Lava signifies expression of anger witch you have kept too long inside.

Lavender is a symbolic of healing.

Lawsuits forewarn that your rivals can be publicly defaming your character.

Lawn signifies pleasure and well-being.

Lawyer-You can have help if you only ask or need.

Lawn Mother-You need to control your attitudes.

Lazy signifies mistakes in your business.

Leaf denotes guilty that is weighting you down.

Leader represents your ability to assert your ideas.

Leak foretells distress for you.

Leaping-You still need to struggle if you want to get your targets.

Learn signifies ever-ending interest.

Leather-Are you still seeking protection from elements?

Leaves-Green leaves signify creativity, fertility and vitality. If the leaves are dry signifies sadness and loss.

Lecture signifies you still continue in your dream to thing something intellectual from your waking life.

Ledge symbolizes sense of freedom.

Leeches-The dream may refer negative emotions that you are sucking out of your vitality.

Lead symbolizes victory and protection.

Left-To dream of the left direction symbolizes the unconscious.

Legs-It is the time to take control again; you are able to navigate through life. If you see other person's legs in your dream-you like to adopt of the ways this person does things.

Lei signify acknowledgment.

Lemonade signifies you to do a lot to pleasure others.

Lemon is a sexual symbol.

Lending is a symbolic of your support system.

Lens signifies need to control better some situation.

Leopard signifies end to the difficulties. If you see a skin of leopard signifies that you have relationship with dishonest person who means only harm.

Leper signifies a rejected aspect of you that is unaccepted by society.

Leprechaun signifies that only from hard work you can get fruits.

Leprosy-Don't be lazy; you are wasting your talents.

Lesbian-If you dream that you are a lesbian signifies to self-love.

Letter foretells opportunities.

Letters symbolizes any object, associated with particular letter.

Lettuce-If the lecture is growing in your dream signifies vitality and pleasure, put if you are eating a lettuce signifies jealousy between you and your lover.

Leveler symbolizes balance and harmony.

Levitation-You should be more realistic.

Liar-If you dream that your lover is a liar forewarns that your disagreeable disposing will turn valued friendship away.

Library signifies hunger for knowledge.

Lice symbolize feeling of guilty.

Lick signifies satisfaction in some minor matters.

Life Guard suggests that you are keeping your emotions well guarded.

Lift represents that you are rising above unpleasant issues.

Light symbolizes clear mind and insight; you may find solution for a problem.

Lighting signifies sudden insight.

Lilac symbolizes disappointments.

Lily symbolizes spirituality and peace of mind.

Lime signifies hard times temporary.

Limousine indicates self-worth and show off and need to impress others.

Limping refers lack of balance in your relationship.

Line symbolizes duality

Linen symbolizes you to see the beauty of the life.

Lingerie is a symbolic of sexuality.

Lions symbolize aggression and power; you know how to overcome difficulties.

Lips are a symbolic of sex and love.

Liquid signifies your ability to conform in different situations.

List-Are you worried of some situation in your waking life?

Listen signifies to pay close attention of what you have been told.

Litter-You need to prioritize aspects of your life.

Liver symbolizes physical disorder.

Living room symbolizes your image and beliefs of yourself.

Lizard is a sex symbol and alternatively symbolizes renewal.

Loan signifies your worries over money matters.

Lobby indicates that you are trying to make some aspect of yourself well-known.

Lobster signifies strength.

Lock signifies your own inability what you want to keep out.

Locked-Are you feeling unaccepted?

Logs signify transformation. If you see a log floating in water represents new opportunities

Lollipops represent pleasant aspects of life.

Long-To dream of anything long refers to penis.

Loom is a symbolic of your destiny.

Loon symbolizes to bring up unconscious wisdom.

Lost-you may feel "lost in life" temporally.

Lottery symbolizes your will to live without worries.

Lotus is a symbolic of expansion of the soul.

Love suggests intense feelings carried from your waking life. If you make love in public signifies you to express your emotions more openly.

Lover symbolizes self-worth; you are feeling complete.

Luggage-In your luggage you carry your desires and needs.

Lumber signifies to rebuild everything.

Lungs signifies stressful situation.

Lust symbolizes lacking in some aspects of your life.

Lute symbolizes faith.

Lynching represents feelings of self-guilt.

Lynx-Always there are more to learn!

Lyre represents joy and happiness.

M

Macadamize symbolizes pleasant journey.

Macaroni symbolizes need to save money.

Mace signifies to you that you don't let emotions rule your actions.

Machinery signifies to repair your relationship.

Madness signifies behaving without control in your waking life.

Madonna symbolizes the mystical mother and also blessings.

Mafia-Don't let others manipulate you!

Magazine-You are getting new ideas-Try to remember what you read from the magazine.

Maggot signifies guilt and impurity.

Magic represents creative mind; put from the negative side magic represents evil.

Magic carpet-You are overcoming physical limitations.

Magnifying glass signifies need to look more carefully to some situation.

Magnolia is a symbolic of beauty and elegance.

Magnolia tree represents need to be noticed.

Magpie-Be careful what you say and do!

Maid-Don't trust help of others; try to be more independent.

Mail represents messages from your unconscious.

Mailbox signifies important information.

Mailman symbolizes communication with others.

Makeup signifies you to try to cover hidden aspect of yourself or increase attention of someone.

Malice signifies you to control your temper.

Mail is a symbolic of materialism.

Mallet-You have a strong mind; use your power to get your goals.

Malpractice signifies you to change your attitudes.

Malt signifies to withdraw from dangerous business.

Man denotes the masculine aspect of you. If you know the man it may reflect your feelings about him. Old man symbolizes wisdom.

Manager indicates to be more organized and efficient.

Mandela symbolizes healing.

Mango symbolizes fertility and sexual desires.

Manicure represents glamour and beauty.

Manna signifies need for spiritual nourishment.

Mannequin represents an extension of your own self.

Manners signifies change of your negative thoughts; pleasant turn in a situation.

Man of war signifies separation.

Manson symbolizes your growth.

Mantilla signifies shame and disfavor.

Manuscript-If you are writing a manuscript signifies fears are not accomplishing your greatest desires.

Map-You are coming to direction that will fulfill your desires.

Maple signifies happiness of life.

Marble-How to polish marble represents perseverance.

March signifies disappointments.

Mare represents your intuition.

Marigold signifies vitality.

Marijuana-To smell marijuana in your dream signifies to check your inner strength; marijuana signifies also ill health.

Mariner-Are you planning to go foreign countries?

Market signifies frugality.

Marmalade signifies illness.

Marriage signifies harmony or transition. Also symbolizes famine or masculine aspects of you.

Mars is a planet of ambitions and new starts.

Marshmallows-If you eat marshmallows in your dream represents lack of self-confidence.

Martyr signifies lack of self-love.

Masochism-Are you suffering for your past mistakes?

Mason signifies social surroundings.

Massacre-You follow ideas of others without any hesitation.

Massage-If you are getting a massage in your dream signifies to lack of sexual stimulation in your waking life. Alternatively your dream suggests you to take better care of your body.

Mast signifies new companionships.

Mastectomy signifies independence.

Master indicates work with much profit and good health.

Masturbation signifies reflection from your waking life that you are not satisfied with your sexual life.

Mat signifies disappointments.

Matches-Something in your life needs ignition.

Mathematics-You need to thing some situation only with rational mind

Mattress-Some relationship needs to take care as soon as possible.

Mausoleum foretells death of close friend.

May signifies times of pleasure.

Mayonnaise signifies disrespect in some relationship.

Maypole dance signifies fertility.

Maze-Are you making the life more difficult that it really is?

Meadow represents security.

Meals-You should give more attention to important matters.

Measurement indicates that you are setting standards for yourself.

Meat signifies animalistic nature and raw emotions.

Mechanic signifies you to overcome your hurting past; you may need some healing treatment.

Mercury is a planet of studies and signifies your efficiency in your work.

Medal signifies that you being recognized from your talents.

Medicine-If you are taking medicine in your dream represents a period of emotional or spiritual healing.

Medieval-You need some updating with your attitudes.

Meditate represents enlightenment.

Medium signifies that you are very sensitive to your instincts.

Medusa signifies cunningness.

Meeting-You are learning to accept new aspects of you. If you are late in some meeting; you may feel unprepared to some situation.

Megaphone represents need to express more yourself.

Melancholy signifies disappointment.

Melon symbolizes misfortune.

Melting-You are melting negative feelings.

Memorandum represents many worries.

Memorial signifies need to confront the past in order to move forward.

Memory signifies that always you can learn from the past.

Men signify highlights of the masculine aspect of you.

Mendicant forewarns interruption in your plans

Mending foretells success to your future.

Menopause-Be little less codependent!

Menorah is a reflection of your religious side.

Menstruation signifies your famine side.

Mercury is a planet of good intuition.

Mermaid suggest (for a woman) doubts of her feminine side.

Merry signifies profitable affairs.

Meshes foretell that your rivals will succeed.

Message signifies changes in your life.

Metal is a symbolic of the inhumane side of society.

Metaphoric signifies rapid changes in your personal life.

Meteor foretells that your wishes will come true.

Mice signify problems with the health.

Microphone-You need to voice your opinions more strongly.

Microwave signifies a quick action person.

Midget-You may feel helpless in some situation.

Midwife signifies illness.

Mildew-You should work more with your feelings.

Military signifies rigid author.

Milk symbolizes maternal instincts and motherly love. If you drink milk in your dream signifies inner nourishment. To spill milk denotes loss of trust.

Milking signifies opportunities that you have.

Mill symbolizes transformation.

Mime signifies you to have problems to show your real feelings.

Mine-Your unconscious is coming to surface.

Minefield signifies many difficulties in your waking life.

Mineral foretells your outlook is coming more effective.

Mining-You are still looking reason for your downfall.

Minister indicates that you have overstepped your boundaries

Mink symbolizes valve.

Miracle signifies your disillusionment.

Mire-Your plans will take more time than you wish.

Mirror is a reflection of you; how do you perceive yourself. To break a mirror in your dream symbolizes unlucky. To see a fogged mirror signifies lack of clarity in a purpose.

Miser indicates a low sense of self-worth.

Missile signifies insecurities about sex.

Missing symbolizes feeling of being of control

Mist signifies confusion.

Mistake signifies that you doubt of yourself in the choices.

Mistletoe signifies much happiness.

Mistress-You may feel neglected in a relationship.

Mixing signifies a blending of the oppose ends of your personality.

Moat-You are trying to block out the hurt.

Mob represents disorganizing.

Moccasins-Walking with the moccasins signifies your ability of treading lightly some situation.

Mocking indicates low-esteem.

Mocking bird symbolizes independence.

Models-If you dream being of a model signifies that you are not trying to be what you really are.

Modest denotes that you have minor concerns about the situation.

Moisturizer is a symbolic of renewal.

Molasses foretell you nice surprises from friends.

Mold signifies new growth.

Moles-Be careful somebody is against you.

Monastery signifies self-reflection.

Money foretells that much success is coming very soon. If you loose money signifies temporally setbacks in your life. If you give money affairs away signifies giving love. If you don't have any money denotes fear of loosing business.

Monk symbolizes a playful personality.

Monster represents part of yourself that you find ugly If you kill a monster in your dream signifies advance better position.

Monument represents valve you.

Moon symbolizes something hidden as well our intuition.

Moose represents vitality.

Mop signifies need to understand your feelings in productive (creative) way.

Morgue is not a good dream; it foretells death.

Morning denotes new beginnings and renewal.

Morph-You need to look the things from other person's perspective.

Mortgage-You surely know how to utilize your energies.

Mosaic-You need to look things from wider perspective.

Moses foretells you better future.

Mosquito signifies that you will try in vain to resist attacks from others. To kill mosquito foretells luck.

Motel represents that you are going through a transitional phase.

Moth signifies character flows.

Mother represents an aspect of your own character. Mother gives guidance and protection; so that you are conversation with your mother in your waking life. If your mother is calling you denote not to run away from responsibilities.

Mother in law foretells that after disagreement things will be resolved in a pleasant matter.

Motorcycle symbolizes your desire to freedom. If you are speeding with a motorcycle denotes that you are moving too fast.

Mountain Lion symbolizes grace. Mountains denote higher reality of consciousness and spiritual truth. If you are climbing a mountain signifies your ambition.

Mourning-If you are mourning in your dream signifies your need to clear old experiences and make way for new life.

Mouse forewarns illness.

Mousetrap-To see a mouse caught in a trap signifies that you will fall into the hands your own rivals.

Mouth signifies that you have said something that you should not.

Mouthwash symbolizes because you couldn't shut your mouth so now you have to "wash your mouth".

Movement represents your ability to adapt to the changing environments that you find yourself in. You know how to express your feelings. Movie-You are watching life pass you by. If you are playing in a movie foretells a new role in your life.

Moving signifies your desire for a change and independence.

Mud suggests that you are involved in a sticky situation.

Muff symbolizes good luck.

Muffins-To eat muffing in your dream signifies pleasure and expensive things in life.

Mulberries-If you eat mulberries in your dream forewarns of disappointments.

Mule symbolizes stubbornness. If a mule kicks you in your dream foretell unhappy marriage.

Mumps symbolizes pent up frustration and anger.

Murder-If you are committed a murder denotes end of bad habits, put if you are a murderer denotes that your feelings have been killed from some relationship.

Muscle signifies power and strength.

Museum symbolizes your history of yourself. If you are in a museum symbolizes you to have an opportunity to renew values of life.

Mushroom signifies illness. If you eat mushrooms in your dream forewarns of disgraced by love.

Music is a positive way to express your feelings.

Musical instruments symbolize talent to communicate with others.

Musk signifies that from unexpected surface comes much happiness.

Mussels foretell that soon you will have much pleasure in your life.

Mustache signifies that you hiding an aspect of yourself (if you don't have a mustache in your waking life).

Mustard symbolizes good luck and wealth.

Mute-You are afraid to say something for fear of being criticized.

Myrrh symbolizes pleasant surprises.

Myrtle symbolizes happiness and prosperity.

N

Nail-To see nails in your dream signifies hard work and little money. If you are hammering your nails symbolizes an ability to drive a hard bargain.

Naked is a very typical dream, symbolizes fear that your secrets will be found out and exposed about your actives and misjudgment.

Name-If you forget somebody's name in your dream suggest that you have forgotten your true self or your family roots.

Nap signifies to you to need a break; take some time off.

Napkin signifies cleanliness.

Narcissus represents vanity; symbolizes also diving love.

Narrow is a symbolic of female sexuality.

Native American symbolizes freedom and liberty from cultural and society restraints.

Nativity signifies you are awarded of your abilities.

Nature symbolizes freedom and renewal.

Nausea symbolizes your suffering from a sickening situation or condition in witch you are trying rid yourself off.

Navel-Miles usually dream of navel because it symbolizes the bonding to their mother.

Navy symbolizes need for organization. If you are rescued by navy person foretells of assistance from a authorial source.

Nazi-You may feel that others are putting you down.

Nearsighted forewarns of unwelcome visitors.

Neck symbolizes the relationship between your body and mind. If your neck is injured signifies separation between your heart and body.

Necklace signifies unsatisfied desires; it is also a symbolic of your intelligence.

Necktie symbolizes unfinished business to tend to.

Need-If you are in need in your dream signifies the danger loosing your fortune through gambling.

Needle is a symbolic of emotional and physical pain. If you are treading a needle it may have sexual connection.

Negligee symbolizes your suggestiveness.

Neighbor signifies enjoyment.

Neighborhood represents sense of community.

Nephew represents some aspect of you.

Neptune is a planet of inspiration and devotion.

Nerd symbolizes ineffectiveness.

Nervous-Are you experiencing some self-doubt?

Nervous Breakdown indicates that you have difficulties trusting your own judgment and decisions.

Nest symbolizes new opportunities and if the nest is full of eggs symbolizes good fortune

Net signifies complicated life.

Nettles signify difficulties expressing you.

New-You are trying new identity. To dream of anything new in your life is connected what is new in your waking life.

News signifies you try to remember what kind of news you have dreamt, good or bad news.

Newspaper-You are seeking knowledge answer to a problem. The dream also signifies your need to express yourself.

New Year is always a new beginning and signifies prosperity and hopes.

Niche-Maybe your dream is guiding you toward place of security.

Nickname represents memories.

Niece represents some aspect of yourself that you need to acknowledge within yourself.

Night symbolizes death, rebirth and new beginnings.

Nightclub symbolizes reflect of your social life.

Nightgown represents some aspect of you.

Nightmare denotes failure and problems in health.

Nimbus signifies deep spiritual progress.

Ninepins forewarns you to select your companions carefully.

Nipples signify you're sexually inadequate.

No represents your need for own decisions, any case not to please others. (Strictly faithful for own truth)

Noise signifies unexpected; maybe something is confusing you in waking life and you can burst through a barrier that makes you afraid.

Noodles signify desire.

North signifies moving forward in life.

Noose symbolizes fears of loosing independence.

North Pole symbolizes that transformation has completed.

Nose signifies energy and intuition and curiously- "Don't put your nose everywhere".

Notary denotes probable lawsuits.

Novel signifies new opportunities in your life.

Nuclear Bomb signifies loss of control. Alternatively maybe your life has chaos someway.

Nugget is a core of knowledge.

Numbers indicates some personal significance, put also every number has special meaning:

0   symbolizes feminine.
1   symbolizes unit.
2   symbolize feminine and masculine.
3   are connected to mother, father and a child.
4   symbolize the wholeness of personality.
5   symbolize 5 fingers.
6   is a symbolic of Star of David, put also connected to sexuality.
7   symbolize 7 days of week.
8   symbolize spiritual wholeness.
9   are connected to 9 months of pregnancy.
10 symbolize the commitments.
11 are connected to 2 men.
12 symbolize the 12 months of year.
13 are connected to circulation of the moon. Some people believe number
13 brings bad luck, I personally believe it brings good luck.

Nuns-If a woman is dressed as a nun signifies unhappiness of her current situation. Also nuns symbolize purity and chastity.

Nuptial foretells engagement and good luck.

Nurse—If you see a nurse suggest you take more care of yourself.

Nursing signifies that you are nurturing a hidden aspect of yourself.

Nuts signify confusion- "Don't tell nuts".

Nymph symbolizes innocence and purity.

O

Oak Tree symbolizes stability and wisdom.

Oar signifies that you are able to navigate through life based on the skills you've learned.

Oasis signifies inner fears and overwhelming conditions.

Oath symbolizes disharmony in your present situation.

Oatmeal-If you are eating a oatmeal signifies that you are well-grounded.

O symbolizes simple life.

Obedience symbolizes new spiritual enlightenment.

Obelisk-It may have phallic implications.

Obese signifies your helplessness in some situation. You need to find way to protect yourself and find a solution.

Obituary represents end to your old attitudes.

Obligation signifies good luck in business undertakings.

Obscene signifies aspects of you.

Observatory symbolizes your high aspirations.

Obsession signifies your need to rest that you can move forward.

Obstacle signifies lack of self to find a decision in some situation.

Occultist-There is some wisdom that you need to add to your daily life.

Ocean symbolizes your emotions, spiritual refreshment and renewal.

Octagon symbolizes a spiritual reawakening.

October signifies pleasure and success.

Octopus-Don't be too much optimistic in your relationship.

Odor signifies memory from your past.

Offence represents spiritual conflict.

Offering signifies hypocrisy.

Office symbolizes your status.

Officer signifies your seeking for better status in life.

Ogre signifies self-criticism.

Oil signifies to you to show your emotions more smoothly.

Oil Spill-You may feel problem in your relationship.

Ointment signifies a healing process.

Old-There is something in your past that needs to incorporate into your current life.

Olives symbolizes faithful friends.

Omelet signifies decent that will be used against you.

One-eyed symbolizes you one-way attitudes.

Onions symbolizes good health.

Onyx is a gemstone of success in business and symbolizes peace of mind.

Opal is a gemstone that symbolizes you needs to learn to show your emotions and your own truth.

Opening signifies new-found inspiration entering in your life.

Opera-Don't be overly dramatic in some situation, opera also symbolizes your social life.

Operation signifies need to take out something from your life.

Opium-Be careful of new opportunities that maybe offering to you.

Opponent signifies a conflict.

Optician—You need to look the things in different perspective.

Oracle-It is good that you are looking forward in positive direction.

Oral sex signifies sexual needs and desires.

Oranges signify health and prosperity, if you see an orange tree. Put if you eat oranges denote loss and separation.

Orangutan-You have a faithful lover.

Orca signifies distrust.

Orchard symbolizes fertility.

Orchestra indicates resolution.

Orchids symbolize beauty and romance.

Ore-Something is still not clear to you, some information needs to dissected in order to be understood.

Oran represents religious view.

Organist indicates the ability to express you.

Orgasm-You need to relieve some of your sexual tensions.

Orgy signifies desires of your own sexuality.

Orient signifies wisdom and intuition.

Ornament is a symbolic of spiritual love.

Oriole represents love and happiness.

Orphan signifies feelings of loneliness.

Ostrich is a symbolic of truth and justice.

Otter symbolizes good fortune.

Ottoman symbolizes that envious rival will seek to defame you in eyes of your lover.

Outer space represents your creativity.

Outlaw represents the animalistic side of your character.

Oval is a symbolic of your aura.

Oven symbolizes the family love and unselfish nature.

Overcoat denotes that mistakes of others will cause you misfortune.

Overfill represents your incoherent thoughts.

Owl is a symbolic of death.

Ox symbolizes masculine power and famine mystique.

Oxygen symbolizes your energies; put if you dream that you don't have oxygen signifies that you are overwhelmed.

Oyster-If you see oysters in your dream signifies wealth and wisdom.

P

Pacifier represents emotional nurturance.

Pacify-You may pacify someone and you'll be respected of your kindness.

Package represents hidden creative skills.

Packing signifies big chances for you. Alternatively signifies burden that you carry.

Page represents that you are on the rebound from a broken relationship. (Don't run to an other relationship immediately)

Pageant signifies that you comparing yourself too much to others.
Pager-Somebody tries to push you to his beliefs on to you.
Pagoda foretells a short trio.
Pail indicates an improvement in your current situation; put if the pail is empty symbolizes that you will suffer loss.
Pain can reveal and warn about health problems.
Paintbrush symbolizes creativity.
Painting-If you are painting your house signifies that you try to cover something; put if you see painting signifies need for self-expression.
Pairs signify need to balance your life.
Pajamas represents that your life is running out without paying attention what is going around you.
Palace symbolizes success and utilizing energies with full potential.
Pall forewarns bad news.
Pallbearer foretells change in social status.
Pallet-If you are making a ballet signifies separation of lovers.
Palm signifies openness and your generous mind.
Palm reading represents ambition.
Palm tree denotes high aspirations.
Pan represents criticism and anger.
Pancake represents pleasure.
Panda symbolizes your childlike qualities.
Panic indicates lack of control.
Pansy-Don't be too gullible,
Panther signifies power and beauty.
Panties-It reflects a female point of view.
Pantomime-You need to be more careful of your friends and relationship.
Pants signify questioning your role in some situation.
Paper signifies need for new start in your life.
Paperclip signifies need to organize certain aspects of your life.
Papyrus signifies your learning of your past
Parachute signifies need to change habit.
Parade symbolizes passage of time.
Paradise signifies need for spiritual perfection.
Parakeets indicate dependency.

Paralyzed signifies difficulties in expressing yourself.

Paranoia symbolizes your fears to move forward.

Parasite signifies loss of vitality.

Parents symbolize power, love and also aspects of yourself; female and male of your character.

Paris is a symbolic of romance.

Park indicates renewal and need for meditation.

Parking ticket suggests loss of sense of not knowing what you really want from your life.

Parsley represents success and purification.

Partner-You need help of others in order to reach your goals.

Partridge represents temptation.

Party signifies need to relax of regular life.

Passageway foretells new opportunities or relationship.

Passenger signifies lack of control in your waking life; Don't let others decide for your own life.

Passport signifies your identity.

Pastel implies ambiguity in your life.

Pastry signifies that you are enjoying life and repairing its rewards.

Path signifies clarity of thought.

Patient-You are going through some healing process.

Patio represents state of mind.

Pauper signifies lacking of self-worth.

Pavement signifies that you are standing on solid ground.

Paying tells you price of actions.

Paw-signifies to you trusts your own intuition.

Peace indicates resolution to an emotional conflict.

Peach signifies lust and sensuality.

Peacock represents new growth and success.

Peanut butter symbolizes misunderstandings and financial problems.

Pearl symbolizes deeper values and purity.

Peas symbolize minor difficulties.

Pebbles-You may feel hurt of something.

Pedestal-Your ego is coming over-inflated.

Peel signifies shedding away of old ways.

Pelican represents nurturance.

Pelvis is a symbolic of sexual issues.

Pen signifies self-expression.

Pencil signifies temporally impact in a situation.

Pendant-You are feeling emotionally touch by someone.

Pendulum signifies important choice in your life.

Penguin signifies need for inner harmony.

Penis signifies power and fertility.

Pentagram is a symbolic of your spirit to the 4-elements (air, earth, fire and water). It is a symbolic of protection.

Penthouse represents creative and spiritual aspect of you.

Peony represents shyness.

People-To see unknown people in your dream signifies hidden aspects of you.

Pepper gives "the aroma to the life".

Percolator-Don't be in a hurry, you need to thing little more.

Perfume is a symbolic of sensuality.

Perm signifies need to change way of thinking.

Prevent-You need to keep distance in some relationship to avoid from getting hurt.

Petals represents quit.

Pet store-Consider what animal you like to purchase.

Pets represent civilizes instincts, what kind of pet do you have.

Petticoat is a symbolic of conservative.

Pewter signifies that your attitudes are out of date!

Phantom represents guilt or represents memories.

Pharaoh signifies your connection with your spirituality.

Pharmacy signifies to try to find a solution to a problem instead of asking help from outside.

Pheasant symbolizes motherhood and nurturance.

Philanthropic signifies that you are willing to share an important part of yourself for a good purpose.

Phobia signifies fears of your life.

Phoenix is a symbolic of renewal.

Photo album signifies that you are idealizing the past.

Photograph signifies also memories, put it may tell false image of someone.

Piano-If you are playing a piano signifies your need for harmony.

Pickle is a symbolic of sexuality

Picnic symbolizes a joyful life.

Picture signifies permanence in your actions. Also can be Deja vu of some situation.

Pie symbolizes reward from your hard work.

Pier signifies introspect into your unconscious.

Piecing-You are regretting your hurtful words and actions.

Pig symbolizes stubbornness and opulence.

Pigeon-Don't plain others from your own mistakes.

Pilgrim indicates a spiritual journey.

Pill represents your inner harmony.

Pillar is a symbolic of stability.

Pillow represents relaxation.

Pilot-You've complete control of your destination in life.

Pimples signify self-image.

Pin-You need to go out of some hurtful situation or relationship.

Pinball-With patience you will success in your goals.

Pine code symbolizes good luck.

Pine apple symbolizes ambition and good luck.

Pinky finger signifies communication and power.

Pioneer-You are looking for new way to express yourself.

Pipe-If you are smoking a pipe denotes knowledge.

Pirate symbolizes freedom and who defies authority-Don't take riskier ventures.

Pistol is a symbolic of power which by you defends yourself against fear and anger.

Piston symbolizes ambition.

Pit signifies feeling of hopelessness.

Pitcher-Sometimes it is hard to keep the feelings only to you put try to be careful of hidden aspects.

Pixie-You may need help or advice from outside.

Pizza signifies variety; alternatively pizza signifies lack of something.

Place mat foretells a new friendship or love.

Placenta-Don't keep anymore unnecessary burden!

Places-what memories do you have from the place you dreamt because it symbolizes state of mind.

Plaque signifies career problems.

Plaid-You have a conflict with your conservative state of mind.

Plains signify of smooth path a head.

Planet-Try to find out what planet you have seen in your dream; then you can know more of your energies.

Planting signifies optimistic view.

Plants signify potential for growth.

Plastic symbolizes artificial.

Plates signify hunger for life.

Platinum symbolizes success and wealth.

Platter signifies that you are feeling envious.

Platypus signifies shyness in public situation.

Play-You are too much around the work; you must have time for fun also.

Playground-It is heavy to carry all responsibilities; it seems time to relax.

Plough signifies new ides.

Plowing-You are preparing yourself for something new.

Plum signifies vitality.

Plumage symbolizes your need to feel protected.

Plumbing signifies need to release emotions.

Plunge signifies need to take a risk in order to move forward.

Pluto is a planet of rebirth and transformation.

Pocket represents hidden talents.

Pocket knife-A good friend is hiding something from you.

Poetry signifies communications.

Point represents common understanding.

Poison denotes illness and negativity.

Poison ivy signifies jealousy.

Poker signifies careful planning before acting.

Pole symbolizes stability.

Police signifies rules and control.

Political party signifies need to defend your beliefs.

Politician signifies manipulative personality; maybe you try to persuade others to support your ideas?

Pollen signifies sharing character.

Pollution signifies to be careful with your words.

Polo symbolizes life and wealth.

Poltergeist signifies lack of control in your life.

Pomegranate signifies fertility, good health and vitality.

Pound signifies need to thing and rest alone.

Pony signifies undisciplined power.

Pool is connected to emotions, need to wash away the past and maybe you like to dive deeper.

Poor represents feeling of inadequacies.

Popcorns signify that new ideas are popping to your head.

Pope signifies narrow mind ness.

Popular signifies vitality.

Poppy-You have to wit row from past and go on with your life.

Porcupine-You should be more openness to approach your needs.

Pornography-Maybe you are afraid in exposing some aspects of you.

Possessed-You are out of control in some situation.

Postcard signifies need to be more open; it is also connected to social life.

Post office signifies an important message from your unconscious.

Pot signifies frustration.

Potato signifies stupidity.

Potato chips symbolize your overindulgent behavior.

Pot holes signify setbacks in achieving your goals.

Potion signifies misfortune.

Power may try to compensate for a waking situation in which you feel powerless.

Power line represents your struggle for power and empowerment.

Praying is an indication that you should pray more.

Praying mantis-Are you praying on others that you are behaving deviously?

Preacher signifies harboring feelings of guilt and self punishment.

Pregnant signifies a birth of new idea. If you really are pregnant then it represents your anxieties about the pregnancy.

Pregnancy test-A new phase is entering to your life.

Prehistoric signifies that you have outdated ides.

Present-You really need to live here and now!

President symbolizes power and control.

Press-Don't be so self-absorbed, pay more attention to outside word.

Pretzel-Complex issue and you don't know how to deal with it.

Pride-You will be challenged.

Priest signifies spiritual needs, also chastity.

Primrose symbolizes purity and vitality.

Prince symbolizes wishes for romance. I f you are a prince signifies need to feel important.

Princess indicates that you are recognizing your full potential.

Printer signifies need to express you in a way that others understand.

Prism is connected to spiritually.

Prison signifies that for some reason you can't express yourself.

Privacy-You are feeling unprotected.

Prize-You are proud of yourself for your achievements.

Procession signifies that you have to take care of your rights.

Professor signifies that you have prominence in some field.

Prom signifies passage of time.

Propeller signifies spiritual journey.

Proposal signifies long-term commitment.

Prostitute signifies need for sexual freedom.

Protection-You may feel helpless in some situation.

Prune signifies growth.

Psyche represents sensitive side of your personality.

Psychogeneses signifies over controlling.

Pub represents need to relax.

Puddle represents feelings that have been over locked.

Pulling represents your responsibilities.

Pulse signifies sort of anxiety in your waking life.

Pumpkin is a symbolic of female sexuality.

Punch signifies hidden aggression.

Punishment signifies guilt about your actions.

Puppet-Don't let others control you!

Puppy symbolizes carefree nature. Newborn puppies signify new idea is coming.

Purse signifies secrets which are being closely guarded. If you loose a purse signifies loss.

Pursuit-You need to concentrate your efforts in something more worthwhile.

Pus signifies that old attitudes need to be released.

Push implies your need for perfection.

Pushpins signify your overlooking for some situation.

Putty signifies need to be more careful with financial affairs.

Puzzle represents a mental challenge that you need to solve. If you find missing piece represents finding a solution.

Pyramid symbolizes firm foundation, also spiritual awareness.

Q

Quack doctor forewarns to be cautious of people who claim to be what they are not.

Quadrille signifies good news.

Quadruplets signifies better situation in your life after long time of problems you have had.

Quagmire symbolizes boring life.

Quail symbolizes good luck.

Quaker symbolizes spiritual beliefs.

Quarantine signifies that somebody is spreading gossip from you.

Quarrel signifies hidden feelings to that person you are quarreling with.

Quarry-You may dig yourself into an emotional hole.

Quartet represents practically.

Quartz symbolizes union of masculine and famine energies.

Quay foretells fulfilling your wishes.

Queen symbolizes personal growth.

Quest signifies your need to work hard toward achieving your goals.

Question signifies self doubt

Quiet signifies your need to be alone and rest.

Quilts signify pleasant and comfortable times.

Quinine-To take quinine foretells an improvement in health.

Quinsy denotes discouraging employments.

Quintuplets represent connection between male and female.

Quote signifies that you are respecting your abilities.

Quoits foretells engagement.

R

Rabbits foretell good luck, to dream of white rabbit symbolizes faithfulness of lover.

Rabies denotes unexpressed hostility.

Raccoon signify false friends.

Race-This kind of dream is revealing your competitive nature.

Race car symbolizes your fast life style.

Racism signifies to you refuse of to be dismissed.

Rack signifies your self doubt.

Racket symbolizes disappointments.

Radar symbolizes message from your unconscious.

Radiant signifies purity and enlightenment.

Radio-If you listen to the radio represents a message from your unconscious.

Radish-To see a radish in your dream signifies prosperous business and good friends.

Raffle signifies your need to be more charitable.

Raft signifies still hard work ahead.

Rage symbolizes that you need to work empowering your inner strengths.

Rags symbolize your cleaning old habits.

Railroad signifies need to create other possibilities.

Rain symbolizes fertility and renewal. If you are watching to rain symbolizes love and good luck.

Rainbow symbolizes good fortune and much success.

Raincoat represents your pessimistic outlook and that you are not able to face the nastiness.

Raisings signifies negative forces try to ruin your optimism.

Rake-Don't wait that others will do your work.

Ram signifies impulsiveness. If the rams are pursing you forewarns misfortune.

Ramp is a symbolic of your ambition.

Ranch signifies concerns about money.

Rape indicates vengeful feelings toward the oppose sex.

Alternatively signifies your violated feelings in some way.

Rapids signify intense feelings.

Rash signifies frustration.

Raspberry-If you are eating raspberry foretells gossip that is being spread about you.

Rats forewarns illness and unworthy thoughts that you are keeping to yourself.

Rattle symbolizes tranquility.

Raven symbolizes misfortune.

Razor signifies that some situation needs smoothing out.

Reach is a symbolic of desire that you will try to reach.

Reading signifies your need to study before an important decision.

Reapers denote pleasure.

Rebirth foretells entering a new state in your life.

Receipt symbolizes enjoyment of life and creativity.

Record represents sensual pleasure.

Rectangle represents stability.

Read head signifies need for more vitality.

Reef suggests you blocking out unconscious material from emerging onto the surface.

Referee signifies an inner battle between your values and values of others.

Reflection indicates how you want others to perceive you.

Refrigerator represents old emotions.

Refugee signifies your feelings emotionally isolated.

Register-To register at a hotel signifies your undertaking some guilty enterprise that gives you much distress

Rehabilitation indicates your re-building something.

Rein deer symbolizes control.

Rejection signifies that you may refuse to accept a situation that is being forced upon you.

Relationship signifies to compare your dream relationship with your waking relationship.

Relief forewarns to evaluate your decisions very carefully.

Religion forewarns misfortune.

Remote control signifies that with a push of bottom you are controlling some situation.

Renovate signifies change of your old attitudes.

Rent-Paying a rent signifies your personal responsibilities.

Repair signifies way out of some situation.

Reptile signifies instinctual nature.

Rescue signifies your trying to find a way to express this neglected part of you.

Reservoir symbolizes repressed emotions.

Resign signifies need for drastic changes.

Resort symbolizes need to re energize yourself.

Restaurant symbolizes your seeking emotional nourishment outside your regular surroundings.

Resume signifies evaluating of your abilities in some situation.

Restrained signifies need to express yourself.

Resurrection signifies renewed energy.

Resuscitate signifies heavy losses.

Retarded indicates feelings of self doubt.

Reunion symbolizes feelings of past that needs to recognize.

Revenge signifies weak character.

Reverend symbolizes that you have to notice other people's needs more.

Revolt symbolizes much pressure around you.

Revolver symbolizes lingering of danger.

Rhinestones signify short-lived pleasures.

Rhinoceros signifies your need to be aggressive to get your goals.

Rhubarb suggests you to go out of some unwanted relationship.

Rib symbolizes misery.

Ribbon signifies pleasant companions.

Rice symbolizes fertility, luck and success. If you are cooking rice symbolizes new responsibilities.

Riddles-Trying to solve a riddle in your dream signifies that your patience will be tasked.

Ride an animal signifies direction of your life.

Right represents rational thoughts.

Ring symbolizes your beliefs and responsibilities; it can be also a commitment to relationship.

Ring master symbolizes that you are putting things in order, organize everything to go forward.

Ringworm symbolizes illness.

Riot signifies a loss of your individuality.

Rising-If you rising to the air signify relaxation from stress. It is also a symbolic of wealth.

Ritual—Forget your old attitudes and let fresh ideas blow to you.

River-Clam-flowing River signifies joy and happiness. If the river is raging signifies loss of control. Gypsies believe that calm flowing river forewarns of problems and raging river foretells good luck in business.

Roaches signify longevity.

Road-First of all try to notice what kind of road it is and where are you going. If you see unknown road signifies new unsure project. If you see a bumpy road signifies difficulties. Straight road signifies success. Gypsies believe that bumpy road forewarns of false friends. Road rage signifies need to find better way to show your feelings if you don't want to hurt someone.

Road sings represent advice from your unconscious. Try to understand the sign.

Road block-You have to be more diligent to overcome the obstacles.

Road runner signifies your way to go from action to another.

Roast symbolizes secrets.

Robbery signifies somebody taking credit from your hard work.

Robe signifies personal issues that you need to confront.

Robin signifies new growth.

Rocket is a male sexual symbolic.

Rocking signifies your view of way you are working.

Rocking chair symbolizes contort.

Rocks signify stability.

Rodeo signifies primal urge.

Roller Blades symbolizes freedom.

Roof symbolizes a barrier between two states of consciousness, mentally and beliefs. If you are falling from the roof signifies that your plans are not in solid foundation. If you are on the roof signifies success.

Rooks signify that you are not happy with your relationship.

Room represents your various aspects of your personality; notice how comfortable the rooms in your dream are. Gypsies foretell that room where you sleep signifies financial problems, hotel room forewarns of illness and dark room loss of money and also bathroom sickness.

Rooster signifies cockney ness.

Roots denote your family ties and bolds.

Ropes-If you climbing up a rope signify success and down signifies disappointments.

Rosary symbolizes satisfaction.

Rose push foretells of period of prosperity.

Rosemary symbolizes sadness.

Rotten-Don't loose your potential.

Rouge signifies that you will obtain your desires even through decertify ways.

Round table symbolizes wholeness.

Rowboat symbolizes hard work.

Rowing signifies that you are doing the things hard way; the symbolic can be also spiritual progress.

Rubber represents your adaptability.

Ruby is a gemstone of strong love, spiritual enlightenment and strong creativity.

Rudder foretells a new friendship.

Rug foretells an advice "you can't change the reality".

Ruins represent destructing personality.

Ruler suggests that don't make fast decision or judgment from anybody.

Rum-You have pleasure and over indulgence.

Runaway signifies that you are dealing with acceptance.

Running signifies that you are not taking responsibility for your actions. If you are trying to run put you can't signifies lack of self-esteem.

Rush signifies you are putting too much pressure on yourself.

Rye symbolizes prosperity.

S

Sabotage-Old ways of thinking needs to rid of.

Sack symbolizes womb.

Sackcloth represents humbleness.

Sacrifice signifies your tendency to punish yourself.

Sad signifies to try to dwell on the negative.

Sadism represents childhood anger.

Safari represents need to get out of civilizing.

Safe signifies secrets.

Saffron signifies false friend, put if you are using saffron in food signifies a solution to your problem.

Sage signifies frugality.

Sailboat foretells success.

Sailing on calm water signifies your ability to handle your life put to sail against the wind signifies difficulties.

Sailor represents your wish for freedom.

Saint represents a holy message.

Salad represents your connection to the nature and vitality.

Salamander signifies good luck and good health.

Salami signifies problems with sexual life.

Sale represents opportunities.

Salesperson signifies need to include something to your life.

Saliva is connected to your sexual life.

Salmon signifies ability to active success.

Salon indicates your conscious; notice how your salon is designed.

Salt represents flower of the life and increased ingrown in your life.

Salt pepper signifies your experiencing a tremendous grief quite soon.

Salve denotes that you will overcome your struggles (if the salve is applied on you).

Samples signify opportunities.

Samurai symbolizes honor and duty.

Sand signifies change of attitude.

Sand castle denotes that it is newer on solid foundation; your plans are not clear.

Sandals signify an open and understanding person.

Sand paper signifies to smooth some situation.

Sandwich signifies ability to do things fast; also a fast compromise.

Santa Claus denotes to show your love to the dearest and nearest ones.

Sap signifies vigor.

Sapphires are gemstones of understanding your conscious. It is also stone of spiritual enlightenment and protection.

Satan denotes environment of evil workings.

Satellite symbolizes global connections.

Satellite dish signifies global awareness.

Saturn is a planet of lesson of life; how do you understand yourself and reasons of understandings.

Satyr denotes need for sexual freedom.

Sauce signifies intellect; notice what aromas you have in the sauce.

Sauna signifies purity and relax ion. Also need to rid of negatives from your life.

Sausage symbolizes material valves put more refers to sexual tension.

Savanna signifies different experiences in your life.

Savings symbolizes your feelings of financial problems.

Saving Bonds represents responsibility.

Saw symbolizes diligence.

Saw dust symbolizes emotional wound.

Saxophone represents need for expression.

Scaffolding signifies something unusual in your life

Scale signifies need to find balance in your decision.

Scallop symbolizes female sexuality.

Scale coat signifies that you have to take responsibility from actions of other.

Scar symbolizes painful memories.

Scarab represents immortality.

Scarecrow symbolizes crisis.

Scared signifies lack of control.

Scarf signifies need to learn to express emotions.

Scepter represents individual power.

School—You maybe go through spiritual learning.

School Bus signifies life journey and your need to growth personality.

Scientist signifies eccentricity.

Scissors signifies control in your waking life.

Scooter signifies your enjoining speed and power.

Scorpion is a symbolic of death and rebirth. It also signifies bitter words against you.

Scratch signifies frustration.

Scream signifies your feelings that you have pent up inside.

Screw-You have to notice small details to mach everything together.

Screwdriver signifies need to hold some situation together.

Scroll represents hidden knowledge.

Sculptor signifies your ability to reach your goals.

Sculpture-It is sometimes difficult to you to accept facts.

Sea is the world of emotions, notice if the sea is calm or stormy.

Sea evils signify that you should leave something behind you.

Sea horse signifies power of unconscious in different perspective in life.

Sea urchin symbolizes your need for help in some situation.

Sea food signifies you're fulfilling of unconscious.

Seal symbolizes good fortune and spiritual understanding.

Séance represents your intuition, information within your unconscious.

Search signifies need to find solution to a problem.

Seashells symbolize your protection against emotional hurts.

Sea sick signifies emotions that are wailing you down.

Seasons represents passage of time.

Sea weep signifies you to trust your instincts.

Secret symbolizes hidden power.

Secretary signifies your need to have more order in your life.

Sedate signifies your avoiding some responsibilities.

Seduction symbolizes sexual desires.

Seed symbolize fertility and potential.

Seizures signify to try to control more your life.

Selling represents changes; better future is waiting for you.

Seminar symbolizes need to understand more in some situation.

Senile-Don't be lazy, you have useful talents.

Separation signifies that your feelings are pulling you to oppose direction.

Serpent signifies intellectual power.

Settle—You can't do everything alone, you have to give some responsibilities to others and also remember to relax.

Sewer symbolizes need to repair some relationship.

Sewing machine denotes economizing in difficult times.

Sex-It can be harmless fantasy; put it can tell much of your desires.

Shack represents your undeveloped self.

Shadows signifies a creative aspect of your self which you don't yet recognized

Shaking is a symbolic of fear and ridding of old habits.

Shaman signifies a spiritual messenger who represents wisdom.

Shampoo represents desire for new image of you to others.

Shapes signify clearer understanding of things.

Shark represents feelings of anger; it may be aspect of you.

Sharpen suggest your need to be flexible in your thinking.

Shave signifies changes in your life; alternatively it is a code for self-punishment.

Shed suggest you not to waste potential.

Sheep suggest you not to follow others; try to be more individual with your thinking.

Sheet music signifies desire for harmony.

Shield symbolizes spiritual protection.

Ship signifies aspect of emotions and unconscious. If the ship is sinking signifies that your life is out of control.

Shipwreck signifies difficulties to express feelings.

Shirt refers to your emotions in some situation.

Shiver signifies highlight of your guilty.

Shock signifies sudden new awareness.

Shoes represent your approachable to life. If you are not wearing any shoes signifies that you have a low self-assurance. New shoes symbolize success and old shoes signify hard work.

Shooting indicates that you have set a goal and your plans will success. If you are shooting someone signifies hidden anger to that person put if somebody shuts you signifies feelings of being victimized in some situation.

Shooting star is a symbolic of good fortune and your wishes will be fulfilled.

Shore is a meeting place of conscious mind and unconscious.

Short signifies need for freedom and signifies your mixture nature.

Shot—If you are shot in your dream represents self-punishment (you may have feelings of quilt.)

Shoulders symbolize responsibility and also ability to nurture others.

Shovel signifies your trying hard to solve a problem.

Shower is a symbolic of forgiveness and signifies need to wash your past away.

Shrimp seems that you feeling insignificant.

Shrine signifies that you are loosing too much energy for something in your life.

Shrink signifies lack of self-esteem.

Shroud symbolizes end for something

Sibling symbolizes unresolved issues.

Sibling Rivalry suggests feelings of doubt.

Sick signifies some part of you needs healing; it also signifies self-pity.

Sickle is a symbolic of hard work.

Side work signifies direction of life, need for changes.

Side ways signify to be more direct.

Sieve signifies wise decisions.

Sing indicates to pay more attention to what sing says-you need guidance in your life.

Signature symbolizes your inner agreement for a particular situation.

Silence signifies your ability to express yourself.

Silk—If you are wearing silk in your dream suggests prestige.

Silo-You are wasting too much money for nonsense.

Silver symbolizes intuition and feminine aspect of you.

Singer indicates clarification of the human spirit.

Singing signifies that you are uplifting others with your positive attitudes.

Sink-Clean up the past feelings and be ready for a new positive start.

Sirens signify that some situation is giving you much stress.

Sister symbolizes some aspect of your relationship with her. If you don't have a sister than it signifies that you need to active within yourself.

Sister in law signifies characteristics in her that you find within your own self.

Sitting symbolizes that it is time to start to do things.

Side according Freud signifies the sire of penis (own or lover)

Skateboard signifies independence and your ability to make difficulties looking easy.

Skating signifies that you are utilizing your energies toward your goals.

Skeleton symbolizes undeveloped thoughts.

Sketch signifies recognizing some aspect of you.

Skiing signifies your pushing yourself to some mental test.

Skin represents shield of inner self.

Skinless-You need to find out the truth of yourself and others.

Skipping symbolizes that you have skipped something important.

Skirts signify the signals you are sending out.

Skull symbolizes the secret of the mind, symbolizes that you are keeping something hidden.

Skunk symbolizes that you driving people of your company.

Sky denotes freedom of expression "only the sky is limit".

Skydiving signifies that you need to realistic of your expectations.

Skywriting represents a spiritual message.

Slap indicates that you are feeling betrayed.

Slave symbolizes that you are not taking charge of your life.

Sled signifies your fun-loving nature.

Sledge hammer signifies that you have to break down the values that you have created around you.

Sleeping except signifies peace of mind; it may also suggest that you are not aware of the conditions around you.

Sleeping bag represents protection.

Slide signifies that you have lost your grip on some relationship.

Slip-Don't force yourself to do things that you really don't want to.

Slippers signify comfort and being lazy.

Sloth is a symbolic of lack of ambition.

Slow motion symbolizes hard stress that you are going through in your waking life.

Slugs indicate that you are going slowly toward your goal.

Slums symbolize crumbling ideas.

Small signifies unworthiness and if you dream that you are smaller than everybody suggest that you have low self-esteem.

Smell signifies memories from your past.

Smog signifies negative emotions.

Smoke tracks signify a warning from your unconscious.

Smoking signifies a conflict with your emotions.

Smuggling indicates that you are feeling denied of something.

Snails signify that you have to trust your own feelings.

Snake symbolizes false around and positively transformation.
Snake is also connected to sex.
Sneakers indicate satisfaction with you.
Sneeze signifies happiness.
Sniper signifies anger—try to take your anger away in healthy way.
Snorkeling signifies need to understand your past memories and
what you have to learn from them.
Snow signifies unexpressed emotions; if you see dirty snow in your
dream signifies situation has been tinted. If you are watching snow
falling signifies spiritual peace.
Snowboarding signifies that you are utilizing your skills.
Snowman signifies frigid emotions.
Soap indicates to wash your past memories away.
Soaring symbolizes freedom after burdening situation.
Soccer is a symbolic of your competency. According to Freud
sports are an aggressive act of sex.
Socks indicate your flexibility of understanding.
Snowball-You are realistic with you capacitive.
Sol symbolizes growth and fertility.
Solder signifies that you are ready to defend your opinions.
Soon signifies your youthful part of yourself. It can be also
mirroring from your waking life
Songs signifies good health and wealth.
Soot-Are you afraid from some part of you?
Sore consider the body area where the sores are. Also you may
have sore emotions.
Sorority signifies chances to social life.
Sound signifies comfort and healing.
South signifies love and warmth.
Sowing signifies new beginnings.
Spa signifies your inner need for healing process.
Space represents independent thinking.
Spaceship denotes spiritual journey of self-development.
Spades symbolizes author.
Spaghetti signifies feelings to end some situation.
Sparrow represents inner dignity.
Spark symbolizes new beginnings.

Speech symbolizes your need to vocalize your thoughts; put the symbolic can be also fear of speaking in public.

Speed forewarns of dangerous situation.

Sperm signifies to growth.

Sphinx signifies fear of unknown.

Spice signifies to look at a situation from other perspective.

Spider symbolizes controlling force and advices you not to put your nose to a tempting situation of somebody.

Spill-If you see a spill in your dream signifies carelessness.

Spindle represents vitality.

Spiral signifies creative power.

Spirits signifies your fears of death.

Spit represents anger.

Splash-If you are splashed with water signifies revitalizing.

Spleen signifies lighten up.

Splinter—Don't let petty things upset you.

Spoiled signifies you to take care of your emotional needs.

Sponge symbolizes that you are sponging off someone from your life.

Spool signifies need for order.

Spoon signifies your need for nourishment.

Sports according to Freud's attitude about sex as an aggressive act; put sports signifies also revitalizing, relaxing and learning rules and talents.

Spotlight signifies your need to be noticed.

Spring is a symbolic of growth, fruitfulness and virility.

Sprinklers represent rejuvenation.

Sprinkling symbolizes birth of something new.

Spy-If somebody is spying on you forewarns that you are being watched.

Square symbolizes solidity.

Squeeze symbolizes unprofitable business.

Stab signifies your struggle with power.

Stadium signifies you to be more aggressive that you can get what you want.

Staff symbolizes a spiritual journey.

Stag represent agility.

Stage represents your behavior and relationship with others.

Stain indicates reversible mistake in your life.
Stained glass signifies spiritual healing and enlightenment.
Staircase symbolizes transformation.
Stallion symbolizes courage and independence.
Stalk symbolizes your power overcome problems.
Stamps symbolize communication.
Standing-Are you proud of something?
Staples signify need to keep things in order.
Starfish suggests a period of healing.
Staring represents your passivity.
Star of David is a symbolic of union of heaven and earth.
Static signifies that you know how to handle things.
Station wagon signifies your family issues.
Statue symbolizes lack of communication. It may represent also someone you idealize.
Statue of liberty signifies your cultural liberty.
Stealing represents unfulfilled goals.
Steam represents your anger of something.

T

Table represents your social unity; It signifies also your family connections. If you are setting the table implies confidence, round table indicates loyalty. Gypsies believe that dreaming from a table foretells prosperity in coming year.
Table cloth signifies quarreling.
Tacks-If you are driving a tack signifies overcoming your rivals.
Tadpoles-For a woman indicates desire to be pregnant.
Tail-To dream tail of animal in your dream signifies much pleasure in some situation to be expected.
Tailor signifies abilities.
Talisman symbolizes your need to be protected.
Talking signifies to consider the feelings; if it is unusual or behavioral reactions.
Tall represents authority and pride.

Tallow-You need to change your careless attitudes and behaving.

Tambourine symbolizes the rhythm of life, you know when to join and when not.

Tame your control over your animalistic urges.

Tangle symbolizes confusion and chaos in your current situation.

Tannery signifies illness.

Tape represents need for restraint.

Tapestry signifies pleasurable surroundings.

Tapeworm forewarns sickness.

Tar indicates you to be more self-recant.

Tarot cards signify your current situation. Wands represent inspiration and psyche. The Sum of Swords signifies determination, strength and faith.

The Cups symbolize emotions, purity and finally the Pentacles denote social influence and connection with the nature.

Tassels foretell that you are reaching your goals.

Taste-If something is tasty in you dream suggest that some action is not enough to sustain you.

Tattoo represents individuality, need to different from others.

Taxes-The dream signifies some self guilt that you feel from the society.

Tent symbolizes temporally changes in your daily routine. Alternatively signifies your insecurity in your current situation.

Termini foretell good fortune over a short period of time.

Terrarium signifies birth of new ideas.

Terror signifies unsolved fears.

Terrorist signifies that your frustrations are giving a pay to your violent tendencies.

Testicles signify power and fertility.

Testify signifies your own truth.

Thanks-If you are thanking someone in your dream indicates accepting some aspect of that person within you.

Thanks giving are a reflection on your life and your sense of community.

It can also be a metaphor indicating that you need thank somebody.

Thatch signifies much discomfort.

Thaw signifies that you are slowly warming person to accept new logos.

Theater signifies much happiness from new companionships.

Thermometer signifies your emotions.

Thief-You may overstep your foundations in some situation.

Thing signifies your ability to perform and do things.

Thimble signifies that you taking care from others more than of yourself.

Thirst to quench your thirst indicates your ability to fulfill your desires.

Thistle-You like to keep distance of people around you.

Thorns symbolize physical suffering.

Threaten denotes your need to stand up in your waking life.

Tea represents contentment in your life.

Teacher suggests that you are seeking some knowledge; alternatively you are seeking some approval.

Teacups indicate spiritual enlightenment.

Teakettle foretells distressful news.

Tears symbolize compassion end emotional healing. Alternatively tears may indicate pain.

Teasing indicates feeling victimized by others.

Teddy bear implies that you need taking care of.

Teenage-You may feel struggling for your independence like "a teenager".

Teeth forewarn to take care of your health and business. To brush your teeth signifies to look after your own interest.

Telegram represents a message from your unconscious.

Telepathy signifies a personal message from your unconscious.

Telephone signifies again a message from your unconscious or may represent communication with others.

Telescope signifies your waiting fore some certain changes.

Television represents your flowing thoughts.

Tempest signifies troubles.

Temptation represents a conflict between your self and desires.

Tenant represents lack of responsibility.

Tennis represents changes, also in love as well in business.

Threshing signifies joy and happiness, also fortune in business.

Threshold symbolizes new beginnings, even marriage.

Throat symbolizes ability to express. If you have a sore throat signifies that you need to swallow your pride.

Throne symbolizes power and author.

Thumb is a symbolic of ability.

Thunder symbolizes anger and aggression.

Tiara symbolizes mystique.

Tick-You need to go away from a relationship which is sucking all your energy.

Ticket signifies new possibilities; if you loose a ticket denotes confusion.

Tickle signifies that you are taking the life too much seriously.

Ticks signify that your job is sucking all your energy.

Tidal awe-you need to find way out from negative emotions that are overwhelming you.

Tides symbolize energy; low tides indicate loss of energy.

Tie represents your relational bonds.

Tiger represents your ability more of leadership role. Also signifies female sexuality.

Tightrope forewarns to be careful in some situation.

Tights signify exposing aspects of your self.

Till is a symbolic of opportunities.

Timber symbolizes prosperity.

Time-If you dream that you don't have time enough signifies stress and fear.

Tin represents mental and intellectual expiation.

Tipsy signifies carefree nature.

Tiptoe signifies emotional stress.

Tires symbolize emotional awareness and you know how to go from situation to an other.

Titans signify control of your own destiny.

Toads signify that you are trying to hide your true self.

Toaster signifies ability think fast.

Tobacco-If you are a smoker represents your need for calm put if you are not a smoker signifies that you are trying to escape life's problems.

Toe sin-If a toe sin begin sounded in your dream signifies that you will win over an argument.

Toddy signifies events that you will change all your life.

Toes signify your path in your life and how you deal with minor details of life.

If you hurt you toe in your dream signifies of your anxiety about moving forward.

Toilet symbolizes releasing of feelings, something that is useless.

Tomb denotes a venture into parts of your personality which has been forgotten. To dream that you are trapped into a tomb suggests that you still are feeling trapped by past pain.

Tongue represents your self-expression.

Tools represent your self-expression, according to Freud tools are symbols of the penis and tools being used are symbol of intercourse.

Toothbrush signifies worries about how others perceive you.

Toothless signifies illness that will be setback of your inability to reach your goals.

Toothpicks indicate your falls.

Top-To dream that you are on the top signifies aspirations.

Topaz is a gemstone of balance.

Topless-You may invite love to your life.

Torch represents ability to success.

Torpedo—To see a torpedo in your dream you may experience some emotional out burns. If you are in a tornado you feel emotionally out of control.

Torrent signifies unexpected trouble.

Torso symbolizes pride.

Tortoise-You need to take a step that you can go forward in your life.

Torture signifies helplessness in some situation.

Totem pole is a symbolic strength and power.

Touching signifies need for contact.

Tourist-If you a tourist in your dream indicate feelings of unsure of surroundings.

Tourniquet signifies feelings of drain.

Towel signifies new starts.

Toy box signifies unresolved issues from your childhood.

Toys signify playful attitudes.

Trail signifies need to connect with some aspect of your self.

Tractor signifies your ingenuity.

Trade symbolizes good luck in business.

Traffic-You feel frustrated in your surroundings.

Tragedy forewarns of disappointments.

Trailer-Your burden is very heavy this moment.

Train-If you are in train in your dream signifies direction of life. If you are in train wreck suggests that you may be lacking of self-confidence.

Training signifies your desire to change your life.

Traitor signifies that you feel ashamed of something you've done.

Tramp signifies to release some heavy burdens. Tram poling signifies resilience.

Trance signifies need to open hearth to others.

Transformation signifies to learn to adjust situations.

Transplant symbolizes need for new start.

Transsexual is a symbolic of famine and masculine roles of your self.

Transparent signifies an ability to see through people.

Trap suggests you to leave old habits.

Trapeze signifies need to relax.

Traveling symbolizes the way you live and behave.

Tray indicates that you spend too much money for nothing.

Treasures signify not to overlook some talent of your self.

Trees symbolize growth and stability. Tree is also a symbolic of self-development and if you are climbing a tree signifies that you are achieving your goals successfully.

Trances signify to be more honest with other people.

Trial suggests you to accept you as you are.

Triangle is a symbolic of body, mind and spirit.

Tricycle symbolizes carefree nature.

Trident signifies creative energies.

Trip signifies a disorder in your life.

Triplets forewarn illness and danger.

Tripod symbolizes stability.

Troll—You have to avoid meeting someone in your waking life.

Trousers signify temptation.

Trout symbolizes good luck in business.

Trowel symbolizes heavy burden to carry up and frustration.

Trumpet suggests your subconscious to be aware of something.

Trust signifies self-acceptance.

T-shirt symbolizes relax.

Tsunami signifies overwhelmed emotions in your waking life.

Tulips are symbolic of charity, faith and hopes.

Tunnel-If you inside a tunnel indicate limited perspective. If you see a light at the end of tunnel symbolizes hopes.

Turban-If you have turban on your head you may feel confined by others think is normal.

Turf symbolizes good luck.

Turkey symbolizes foggy future; you need to clear some things.

Turquoise is a gemstone of protection and symbolizes good luck.

Twin lights symbolize that after misfortune the future is looking much better.

Twin signifies dualities and opposes harmony and conflict.

Typing signifies difficulties expressing verbally your ideas.

Typhoid forewarns of false surroundings.

U

U-turn indicates that you changing directions after you have made a mistake.

Ufo signifies you to be more grounded, you are not living in the reality.

Ugly signifies feelings you've rejected.

Umbrella is a symbolic of emotional security.

Uncle represents aspect of your family and signifies to awareness.

Unemployed represents lack of self-worth.

Underground-Your thoughts are pushing subconscious mind.

Undertaker signifies that you need to take more responsibility with the changes of life.

Underwater-Your deep emotions need to overcome for new path of life.

Underwear signifies a private aspect of yourself that you don't want anyone to know.

Unemployment signifies lack of self-value.

Unfortunate signifies just oppose.

Unicorn signifies only one way views.

Rita Hawi

Unknown signifies hidden part of you.
Up signifies inflated ego.
Uproot signifies lack of balance.
Upside-down signifies chaos with your emotions.
Uranus is a planet of independence and individualism; something unexpected can happen.
Urinal signifies disorder in your personal life.
Urination signifies release of negative emotions.
Urn signifies lack of energy.
Utensils symbolize your good will.

V

Vacation-Maybe you really need holiday because it signifies to revitalize yourself.
Vaccination suggests you to overcome your vulnerabilities.
Vacuum signifies feelings of emptiness, you need to rest and revitalize yourself.
Vagina signifies sexual needs.
Valentine signifies need of love.
Valley symbolizes need to be protected.
Vampire symbolizes loosing your virginity or obsessive relationship.
Van-What are you carrying in the van because a van signifies to heavy responsibilities.
Varnishing signifies that you have you done a mistake and how you can cover it now?
Vase symbolizes creativity and also vase is connected to sex.
Vat symbolizes sorrow.
Vatican symbolizes your spiritually.
Vault signifies your potential.
Vegetables signify your vitality and it is also connected to sex.
Vegetation signifies problems that you have to overcome.
Vehicle symbolizes control and power.
Veil represents something that you have to conceal.

Vein-If vein is bleeding in your dream forewarns sorrow.
Velvet signifies honor.
Veneer signifies you to try to be yourself in all situations.
Venereal disease signifies to be hurt in some situation.
Venom signifies hostility from friends.
Venus is a planet of love, fertility and beauty.
Veranda signifies success.
Verdict signifies that you are afraid of your actions.
Vermin symbolizes disappointments and illness.
Vertical signifies high spiritual emotions.
Vertigo signifies your feelings of discomfort in some situation.
Vessels signify hard work.
Vest represents compassion from others.
Veterinarian signifies you to control instinctive behavior more.
Vicar signifies need to spiritual awareness.
Victim signifies emotional hurt.
Victory-Sometimes is good to imagine a victory because it gives motivation.
Video camera-Don't ever mix feelings with decisions.
Video game signifies an ability not to take stress from every problem.
Village signifies balance and respect for traditions.
Vines signify new ideas and spirituality.
Vinegar symbolizes emotional hurt.
Vineyard represents life experiences.
Violated signifies feelings of guilt that are beyond your control.
Violets foretell marriage.
Violin symbolizes love and harmony and playing violin signifies deep emotions.
Viper forewarns of false friends.
Virgin is a symbolic of purity.
Virgin Mary signifies spiritual harmony and forgiveness.
Vise signifies that you feel confused of something.
Vision can be epic dream, try to notice the surroundings and what do you see around.
Visitor foretells a good message.
Vitamins forewarn to take care of your eating habits.
Voiceless signifies lack of self-worth.

Volcano signifies trying to control your emotions
Volleyball represents need for co-operation and sociality.
Volunteer signifies your willingness to help others.
Vomiting signifies need to vomit your negative away.
Voodoo signifies primitive aspect of your self.
Vote-You like to have your voice to be heard.
Voucher signifies new opportunities.
Voyage foretells inheritance.
Vultures signify your experience to reach your targets.

W

Wadding signifies inner fears and need to be protected.
W signifies power to control emotions.
Wafers symbolize something that needs to handle with care.
Waffle suggests you to be more grounded.
Wagers-If you are receiving wages symbolizes reward, put if you
are paying out wages signifies false.
Wagon symbolizes difficulties; it must be hard to drive a wagon.
Wagtail forewarns gossip.
Waif signifies luck in business.
Waist symbolizes a comfortable life.
Waiter-If you are waiting for a waiter signifies better times in the
future.
Wake signifies awareness to your dearest and nearest ones
Walking signifies the way you are moving through life.
Walking stick symbolizes that you need help of others.
Wallet signifies self-identification. If you have lost or stolen a wallet
signifies need to be more careful and cautious of surroundings.
Wall paper signifies need to keep distance from others of your
private life.
Walls signify boundaries and limitations. If you are building a
wall signifies that you have accepted your limitations put if you are
hiding behind a wall signify that you are ashamed of something.
Walnut represents abundance

Walrus signifies your will to be better than others.

Waltz foretells pleasant relationship.

Wand represents influence over others.

Wandering signifies your seeking direction to your life.

Want signifies potential to active.

War signifies conflict and disorder with emotions.

Warden signifies that author can control your behavior.

Wardrobe signifies how you like to show your life to others.

Warehouse symbolizes hidden resources.

Warmth symbolizes unconditional love.

Warning forewarns to rethink your actions.

Warrant-Consider what type of warrant because it usually signifies important decision?

Warrior represents your ability to confront life's challenges.

Warts-Everybody makes mistakes; why it is so difficult to forgive yourself.

Washboard signifies feelings of emotional drain.

Wash bowl foretells joy and happiness.

Washing signifies need to clean up all negative feelings.

Washing machine is also connected to cleaning and solving problems.

Wasp-If you kill a wasp signifies that you are strong enough to keep your ethics and judgment even against the worst enemy.

Waste is a worthless situation; don't waste your energy for nothing.

Watch-If you are looking all the time to a watch signifies controlling every second-Try to be more careless.

Watching signifies lack of motivation put if you are being watched you feel lack of privacy.

Water symbolizes the living essence of the psyche. Clear water signifies stability and balance of emotions. If the water is muddy signifies unclear situations and negative emotions. Water is also a symbolic of spiritually and knowledge and healing.

Water carrier symbolizes fortune and love.

Water lily signifies sorrow.

Water skiing represents freedom.

Water bed symbolizes recognizing your feelings.

Water fall signifies luck and vitality.

Water melon represents feelings of love.

Water mill signifies to utilize your opportunities.

Waves signify decision you have to make soon. If you hear waves crashing signifies relaxation.

Waving signifies need to develop closer friendship.

Way symbolizes the way of life.

Weak signifies need to renew your energies.

Wealth represents rewards of your achievements and work.

Weapon signifies need to defend your emotions; you may have some conflict with your emotions.

Weasel signifies feelings of shame and lack of self value.

Weaving signifies to figure all the picture, collect all the peaces together.

Web represents your social network.

Wedding signifies transition and feeling of independence. If you getting married signifies new beginning and if you are married and you dream of wedding signifies union of your masculine and famine side.

Wedding dress-If you are wearing a wedding dress signifies that you are evaluating your personal relationship.

Wedge signifies support.

Wedlock signifies that you have found yourself in uncomfortable situation.

Weeds signify need to release negative thoughts.

Weeding symbolizes disappointments.

Weevil symbolizes false and loss of property.

Weighting-You are weighting several opportunities and determine the worth of opportunities.

Weight represents self-esteem and burdens of life.

Welcome represents ability to trust others.

Well represents talents that are coming to the light.

Werewolf represents feeling not to trust everything you have been told.

West-Sun is setting to the west and sun symbolizes harmony and opportunities are coming usually in elderly age.

Wet signifies spiritual cleansing and rebirth.

Wet nurse forewarns that you will be widowed.

Wet suit signifies your feelings; wet suit keeps you dry inside and that is why you are feeling comfortable.

Whale signifies good intuition.

Wheat signifies growth and sometimes wheat is connected to pregnancy.

Wheel barrow symbolizes hard work.

Wheels represent continuations and routine.

Whip represents ashamed and guilt.

Whipping boy signifies self-destruction.

Whirlpool signifies emotional repression.

Whirlwind represents chaos and scandal.

Whiskey-If you are drinking whisky in your dream signifies confidence.

Whispering-You need to listen to someone (somebody needs your help).

Whistle signifies end to some situation.

Widow represents independence.

Wife signifies need to solve some problem.

Wig symbolizes false.

Wild signifies a primitive aspect of you.

Wilted signifies wasting your talents.

Wind signifies changes into your life.

Windmill represents the power of your mind.

Window signifies your outlook on life and intuition; try to notice what you can see from the window. Shut windows denotes emptiness of the soul.

Wine signifies celebration.

Wine cellar represents experiences from your past.

Wine glass is a symbolic of pregnancy.

Wings of angel signify to protection and wings of birds are connected to desire of freedom.

Winter signifies gold and frigid emotions. Also winter is a symbolic of misfortune.

Wire signifies your journeys.

Wise signifies your abilities to success.

Wish signifies hopes that yet didn't happen.

Witch is a symbolic of evil. Alternatively witch symbolizes power.

Witness-Some problem needs to be solved put you need to collect more details and try to be careful.

Wizard-Are you trying to exercise your power?

Wolf is a symbolic of mystery and signifies contacts with social situations.

Woman signifies caring nature and love; group of women signify gossip.

Womb symbolizes new birth (also spiritual).

Wood signifies routine or alternatively signifies vitality.

Wood pile signifies misfortune.

Wool signifies warm emotions.

Work signifies the routine of everyday life.

Workshop represents the development of your talents.

World-You have too many responsibilities on your shoulders, let others also do something.

Worm represents lack of self-value.

Wound is a symbolic of distress.

Wreath is a symbolic of completeness.

Wreck indicates lack of energy.

Wrestling signifies need for more order in your life.

Wrinkle is a result of your life experience.

Wrist signifies that you are full of excitement and good energies.

Writing in your dream indicates communication with your unconscious.

X

X-ray symbolizes your founding a solution to your problem.

Y

Yacht is a symbolic of luxury.

Yak signifies that you are concentrating to yourself too much.

Yam signifies celebration.

Yard symbolizes privacy.

Yardstick signifies good judgment.
Yarn symbolizes routine of life.
Yawning signifies temporally lost of your vitality.
Yearn signifies denying yourself of something.
Yeast symbolizes that some new idea gives you energies to fulfill it.
Yelling is a way to release negative emotions.
Yes signifies an acceptance of a decision.
Yellow bird foretells good fortune.
Yin yang symbolizes the famine and masculine.
Yoga symbolizes controlling of body and mind.
Yoke signifies individuality.
Young represents a younger aspect of you.
Yule log signifies optimism for a coming year.

Z

Zebra represents balance.
Zenith symbolizes your ambitions and potential
Zephyr signifies your contentment of life.
Zero symbolizes completeness.
Zinc-If you taste zinc in your dream suggests you to be aware of your health.
Zinnias symbolize joy and happiness.
Zombie symbolizes confusion.
Zoo signifies your feelings of lack of freedom and privacy.
Zoomed prism signifies your primal desires.

References: Dictionary for dreamers, Tom Chetwyn
Robert Langs: The Dream Workbook
Special thanks to H.H Dalai Lama and to: www.astro.fi and my
dear friend Conny Barghoorn and of course to my family.
All the copy rights only to Rita Hawi

Artist profile
I have published my first book in 2002(Conversations with
Shulamit in Hebrew)
End of 2007 Immortal Verses-USA(My evening walk)-my poem
Winter 2008 Centres of Expression, Deep Emotions-my poem
Best Poems&Poets 2007-ELY
Several winnings in poetry contests and the song, Perfect Sense

You may contact Rita Hawi at:

Phone number: 058 4298 723
Fax number: 020 5901 134
Email: riitta@walla.com or riitta.hawi@gmail.com